The Refrigerator Files

A Guide to CREATIVE MAKEOVERS for your LEFTOVERS

Jocelyn Deprez

iUniverse, Inc.
New York   Bloomington

The Refrigerator Files
A Guide to CREATIVE MAKEOVERS for your LEFTOVERS

iUniverse books may be ordered through booksellers or by contacting:

iUniverse
1663 Liberty Drive
Bloomington, IN 47403
www.iuniverse.com
1-800-Authors (1-800-288-4677)

ISBN: 978-1-4502-7029-8 (sc)
ISBN: 978-1-4502-7030-4 (ebk)

Printed in the United States of America

iUniverse rev. date: 11/02/2011

DEDICATION

This book has been written for all the old timers and newcomers in the kitchen, those who, like me, had to learn or are learning from scratch. Out of necessity we cut our fingers, burn our hands, scorch our pans because we need to put a meal on the table. Therefore I hope this little guide will help both the seasoned cook and the neophyte find ways to stretch their budget, along with their imagination, and have fun with all that time spent in the kitchen.

Front cover: family archive photograph of our first house
Back cover: 2010 photograph by Angela Deprez
World War II poster from the Northwestern University Library
http://digital.library.northwestern.edu/wwii-posters/img/ww0870-11.jpg

From a 1943 World War II poster

ACKNOWLEDGMENTS

I would like, first of all, to thank my family for eating their way through all the failed and successful meals I have put before them and for dutifully cleaning their plates. I like to think that an occasional balking was due more to distaste for the ingredient (calf's liver, for example) than for my preparation of it. But then, I was still learning. I am grateful to my husband, André, for suggestions over the years ("Maybe you could vary the menu a little?") and for his patience with my experiments. My daughter, Thé, who was my little kitchen helper from the time she was barely tall enough to reach the table top, has provided many thoughtful insights and endless support. My other three, Charlie, Alex, and Sophie contributed countless hours prepping, doing the dishes, and learning in the process.

My thanks also go to Belden Merims, for her editorial savvy and culinary expertise in helping me put together this book in as reader-friendly a fashion as possible. The team at iUniverse has been tireless in giving me advice and support, and I am most grateful for their patience and cheerful help.

I am also grateful to the cookbook industry for publishing so many fascinating resources. Mine have been many over the years, Irma Rombauer's *Joy of Cooking* still being my bible. My introduction to French cuisine came with the series of *Chamberlain Calendars of French Cooking*. These date back to the 60's but are ideal for the beginner with their no-nonsense simplicity. Julia Child's *Mastering the Art of French Cooking* has been an inexhaustible source of inspiration. Delia Smith's *Complete Cookery Course* helped give a British tilt to some recipes. Betty Crocker's *Cookbook* has been a valuable resource for traditional American cuisine. Exceptionally good ideas can be found in *Bread*, by Beth Hensperger. *The New Larousse Gastronomique* (English version) has given the last authoritative word when in doubt. Not to be upstaged by the wealth of tradition, recipes found on the Internet have sparked many good ideas. The list goes on and on, my kitchen shelf sagging from the weight of valuable publications and my filing bin bursting with newspaper clippings. Please see the Bibliography at the end of the book for a list of books I use frequently.

And last but certainly not least, I am grateful that there are readers out there who are as concerned as I about husbanding their resources and applying their imagination to the most fundamental human activity: eating.

CONTENTS

INTRODUCTION

When I come upon recipes in books, magazines, or newspapers, I am frequently discouraged by the number of special ingredients needed. There are hundreds of books out there designed meet our particular needs or tastes. But what about someone like me, who is daily confronted with the big question, "What can I do with all those leftovers cluttering my refrigerator shelves?" It would be against my Scottish mindset to throw them out. My family has been living for many long years with "garbage salad" or "garbage soup". "Delicious!" is the usual verdict. Furthermore, there is the arrival of an unexpected guest or even a spontaneous get-together that demands a quick response from your refrigerator. With a few basic methods and ingredients, you can brave this challenge by calling on all those leftovers crying out for a second chance.

Most of us deal with our scraps the easy way: we zap them in the microwave and munch our way through the soggy or hardened result and breathe a sigh of relief that we can now start again with something brand new. But what about sprucing up those nutritious odds and ends, which have certainly picked up flavor in their sojourn in the fridge? There are many ways that we can transform them into memorable dishes by incorporating them into some other basic procedure.

When confronted with traces of yesterday's dinner, the first question to ask oneself is, "What *kind* of meal do I need to make? Lunch? Dinner? "Is the weather hot? Cold?" You get the idea. Therefore, this guide's sections have been organized into cooking procedures that lend themselves relatively easily to leftover metamorphosis. Each section starts with a general description of the basic procedure, followed by a few recipes to get you started. These recipes include ones that I have used for many years and also a few I have borrowed in order to highlight a specific leftover ingredient. In this case I have mentioned my source.

The point of all this is to help the reader use resources at hand and not feel that he or she has to run out to the store for a missing ingredient. Also, measurements are not hidebound. You should feel free to vary the proportions according to what you have on hand. As we give you a general idea of proportions, you will learn to wing it. By daring to be creative in transforming your leftovers, you will also be inspired to use odds and ends of fresh produce in new ways. Remember, this is not rocket science. The only prerequisites are a love of eating, the ability to read, and a little imagination.

The presentation of the recipes does not follow the conventional layout, where all the ingredients are listed at the top, followed by the instructions. Here you will find step-by-step instructions as you go along, with the ingredients listed in **bold face** to the right. Just scan the right side of the page to see what ingredients are required.

In the Table of Contents you will find the chapters arranged in the conventional order and the dishes organized approximately in the order in which they would appear on a menu. The Foretaste, an Interactive Guide, which follows, is a new form of index to facilitate your search for an appropriate procedure for your leftovers. Every effort has been made to simplify the steps between the dilemma of what to do with those pesky refrigerator containers and savoring the result of their contents' glorious transformation.

FORETASTE
an INTERACTIVE GUIDE

What Makeovers Can I Create From These Leftovers?

As you open your refrigerator door and are faced with the challenge of all those containers of carry-overs from yesterday's meal, just scan the following guide to help you navigate the many possibilities for their happy enhancement.

APPLES (see FRUIT)

BANANAS (see FRUIT)

BREAD (Stale)
  Canapés, *19*
  Bread Crumbs; use them in
    Fritters, *73*
    Croquettes, *75*
    Fish Turnovers in Filo
    Dough, *80*
    Gratinées (Topping), *81*
    Meat Loaf, *83*
    Fish Loaf, *83*
    Chicken or Turkey Loaf, *84*
    Birds, *85*
    Moussaka, *91*
    Stuffed Vegetable
    Casings, *100*
    Stuffed Eggplant
    Shells, *102*
  Croutons, *137*
  Fried Bread, *138*
  Crouton Turkey or Poultry
  Stuffing, *139*
  French Toast, *13*
  Cheese Melt, *140*
  Hard-Boiled Eggs in Cheese or
  Curry Sauce, *49*
  Meat Patties, *93*

Sweet Puddings, *146*
Bread & Butter Pudding, *146*
Old-Fashioned Bread Pudding, *147*
Cream Desserts, *149*

CAKE (Stale)
  Cream Desserts, *149*
  Baked Alaska, *155*

CHEESE
  Cheese Sauce (Mornay), *10*
  Alfredo Sauce, *11*
  Dips and Canapés, *18*
  Sprinkled on Soups, *23*
  Omelets, *47*
  Frittata, *48*
  With Hard-Boiled Eggs, *49*
  Quiches, *51*
  Soufflés, *54*
  Crêpes, Filling and Sauce for, *62*
  Quesadillas, *69*
  Enchiladas, *70*
  Burritos, *72*
  Chilaquiles, *71*
  Cheese Croquettes, *78*
  Gratinées, *81*
  Shepherd's Pie, *90*
  Chicken and Eggplant
  Parmesan, *94*
  Eggplant & Zucchini Crustless

CORN

CHAPTER 1: BASIC ARSENAL

Before we open that refrigerator door to get started, let's check our shelves to be sure we have a basic arsenal on hand. Following the lists of supplies and kitchen utensils, there are definitions and measurement abbreviations pertinent to *The Refrigerator Files*.

SUPPLIES

THINGS TO STOCK TO BE ABLE TO DRAW ON QUICKLY

Asian sauces	For stir-fry
Assorted dried and fresh herbs and spices	Herbes de Provence, ginger, curry, tarragon, cinnamon, nutmeg*, basil, tarragon, dill, oregano, thyme, cumin, cardamom
Bacon	A great addition to many dishes
Biscuit dough	Home made or store-bought
Bouillon cubes (a cook's best friend!)	Chicken, beef, vegetable, herb, fish (if you can find them)
Canned tomatoes, tomato sauce, tomato paste	
Cheese	A big chunk of supermarket extra-sharp cheddar, Monterey Jack, and/or Swiss cheese
Cream cheese	A useful addition to stretch leftovers in fillings
Dairy products	Eggs, milk, cream or half & half, butter, margarine (stick, not spread), whipping cream (occasionally)
Dijon mustard	This is the most versatile kind of mustard.
Flour and **sugar**	Keep handy a smaller jar of each with a tablespoon in it for quick access.
Fresh produce	Onions, garlic, carrots, celery, parsley, cilantro, lemons. Also, ginger is nice.
Frozen pie crusts	Store-bought if you don't have time to make them

Grated cheese	Buy or make your own.
Honey	Have a large pot of supermarket honey on hand.
Knox unflavored gelatin	Have a box of 4 envelopes on hand. 1 envelope will gel 1cup liquid.
Mayonnaise	If you don't have time to make it, get Hellman's or some other brand with minimum sugar.
Oils	Olive, vegetable (canola if possible), sesame seed (for stir-fry)
Pasta sauce	Any kind
Salsa	Especially if you are into Mexican-style food
Sour cream	You can make your own (see page 140).
Vinegars	Red and white wine, cider, balsamic, rice (for stir-fry)
Wine	White and red
Yogurt	Plain only! Forget the fruited kinds; they contain way too much sugar and are not versatile enough for general cooking needs.

* A word about **nutmeg**: If you can find a small, fine grater, dedicate it to grating only whole nutmegs. Freshly grated nutmeg is an amazingly versatile flavor enhancer.

STAND-BYS YOU NEED TO PREPARE AHEAD OF TIME

Biscuit dough	Make ahead of time and freeze.
Bread crumbs	Dry out your stale bread bits and throw them into a processor or blender. Crumbs made from garlic bread or crackers are nice (see page 137).
Cake, cookie crumbs	Put stale pieces in a Ziploc bag and mash with a rolling pin.
Croutons	See recipe on page 137.

Frozen pie crusts	Make several at a time, roll them, put them in aluminum pans, store in freezer.
Grated cheese	You can make your own in a food processor with hardened scraps.
Hard-boiled eggs	Keep a couple on hand, but watch that they don't spoil after 2-3 days.
Mayonnaise	See recipe on page 33.
Stock	Chicken, meat, fish (see page 23). **Save cooking water from veggies, shrimp, meats!**

KITCHEN UTENSILS

It goes without saying that you have a basic arsenal of kitchen utensils. Nevertheless, here are a few

MUST HAVES

You should have a blender.	Also, a **food processor** is useful but not essential.
A chef's knife	It should be sturdy with good balance between blade and handle. High carbon stainless steel will keep its edge best. Make sure your knuckles don't hit the board when you are chopping.
A knife sharpener	Best is a manual sharpener (in case of a power outage!). A sharpening steel also works.
A paring knife	It should be small and sharp. Best if the handle is a contrasting color to your counter top, so it's easy to spot.
A vegetable peeler	I like the kind that swivels.
A cutting board	The larger the better because you need lots of chopping room. It should be **wooden** because plastic will blunt your knives. To prevent a cutting board from slithering around, put a damp dishcloth under it.

Wooden spoons

You need several kinds. A wooden scraper is useful to keep food from sticking to the bottom of the pan.

Rubber scrapers

I can't have enough of them. They should have wooden handles, as plastic will melt when you rest it on the pan's edge.

Wire whisks

You should have a large and a small balloon whisk. The flat, spiral kind is also useful for mixing in a flat dish.

Spatulas

Again, you need a selection: large, small, stiff, flexible, steel, plastic (for non-stick ware).

Large spoons & forks

Keep handy a couple of old, beat-up metal soup spoons and forks. They have infinite uses.

A slotted spoon

Essential for fishing items out of boiling liquid

A pastry brush

Stay away from nylon bristles; they melt when heated.

A rolling pin

For pie crusts and cookies

Bowls

Another item I can't have enough of. Stock them in a variety of sizes and materials (Pyrex, metal, etc.)

Measuring cups

Again, a selection is useful: Pyrex for easy pouring and microwaving; metal for heating in oven; plastic nests for quick leveling-off.

A colander

The holes should not be too big. Certain ingredients should not sit in metal, so it's good to have a plastic one. On the other hand, metal ones are sturdier. (I have one of each.)

Metal sieves

Stock several sizes. Some ingredients need fine drainage.

Pots and pans

If your cook top is ceramic, make sure your pans have thick, flat bottoms. All your pans should have well-fitting lids.

Oven-proof dishes

Pyrex, metal, enameled cast iron, ceramic: they all have their advantages. Again, you need several sizes.

Ramekins

a.k.a. custard cups

A can opener	Get a manual one; they are quicker and handier (again, think power outage!).
A juice squeezer	A regular, hand-held one is fine.
A grater	The box kind is best, but I also use a flat one for thin slicing. A small one for zest is handy.

And last but far from least (this is your badge!)

An apron	It should be cotton, so you can wipe your hands on it. It should have a bib, a pocket or two, and long ties to wrap around yourself so you can hang a towel or dishcloth from it.

NICE BUT NOT ESSENTIAL

A cleaver	Wonderful for chopping, splitting a chicken, and many other functions. It is *the best* for scooping up your choppings.
A salad spinner	You can always let your salad drain in a colander, but a spinner is much more efficient.
A large ladle	This is a multi-purpose utensil.
An herb chopper	Great for mincing all sorts of ingredients, also for chopping nuts.
A ricer/food mill	A kind of strainer with a disk and a rotating handle that forces food through the holes.
An egg slicer	Great when you want to decorate with neat slices of hard-boiled egg or chop them for a salad.
A garlic press	Saves a lot of chopping and mashing.

MEASUREMENT ABBREVIATIONS

c. = cup (8 oz.)   Tbs. = tablespoon
2 c. = 1 pint   tsp. = teaspoon
2 Tbs. = 1oz.   3 tsp. = 1 Tbs.

TIPS FOR MEASURING FLOUR

Scoop flour out of its container and sprinkle lightly into measuring cup until overflowing. Scrape top with straight edge of knife. Do not jiggle the cup or pack the flour. Dump it into a sifter, add other dry ingredients, and sift into a large bowl.

This method should be used to measure flour for baking. However, in recipes where only a small quantity is required, such as for white sauce (a.k.a. béchamel), just scoop the flour directly out of its container, but level it off by scraping off the excess with a flat surface.

A FEW DEFINITIONS

Béchamel	White sauce or cream sauce
Bouillon cubes	They come in different sizes, but I use Knorr, whose cubes are slightly under ½ oz. each. One cube will make 2 cups of bouillon. Warning: bouillon cubes are salty!
Crème fraîche	Since this is rarely available in the USA, you can make do by mixing equal parts of plain yogurt with heavy cream. It can be used in cream desserts for an extra tangy flavor.
Eggs	"Large" eggs are implied in all recipes.
En cocotte	In ramekins (custard cups)
Flour	Unbleached all-purpose flour is the standard in this book.
Gratinée	A scalloped preparation
Herbes de Provence	A classic French mixture of dried herbs, mainly basil, thyme, rosemary, marjoram, chervil, and bay leaves. Very useful to have on hand, but use it lightly so it doesn't dominate.
Julienned	Cut into short, thin strips
Milk	Generally 1% or 2% fat is recommended. If, like me, you use fat

free, you can enrich it with a little half & half where appropriate.

Roux
Flour cooked slowly in butter or fat to form the base for béchamels or soups

Sour cream
Generally the store-bought plain, whole, or "light" kind is meant.

Soured cream
This term is used if you want to make your own sour cream. Either let your half & half or whipping cream go sour, or add 1 tsp. lemon juice or white vinegar to 1 cup milk or cream. In this case, you will need to add ½ tsp. of baking soda per cup of sour cream to your ingredients to counteract the sour taste.

Sour milk
The above method for making soured cream also applies to making sour milk.

White sauce
See Béchamel.

Zest
Grated lemon, lime, or orange rind

CHAPTER 2: SAUCES

Before we tackle the approaches to glorifying your leftover cooked food, here are three similar, very basic recipes that should be mastered. You will use them time and time again as the kick-off point for many of the procedures in this book. The first is for **béchamel**, a.k.a. **white sauce**. The second is for **binding béchamel**, which is used as a stiff base for croquettes and dumplings. The third is for **brown sauce**, a slight elaboration of the first.

For a medium or thick **béchamel**, the ratio of shortening to flour to liquid will be designated as **2:2:1**, or **3:3:1** respectively. This means you will be using a ratio of 2 Tbs. shortening to 2 Tbs. flour to 1 cup liquid (milk or stock) for a **medium béchamel**. For a **thick sauce** the ratio will be 3 Tbs. shortening to 3 Tbs. flour to 1 cup liquid (**3:3:1**). This is such an easy operation that you will get used to it in no time. It's my fall-back when I don't know what else to do.

An even thicker béchamel, used for croquettes and dumplings, has the ratio of 3 Tbs. shortening to 5½ Tbs. flour to 1 cup liquid (**3:5½:1**). This is called a **binding béchamel**.

A **brown sauce** follows the same principle as above, but it requires the slow cooking of some chopped vegetables in the shortening and the addition of some other ingredients, plus longer simmering. As a shortcut, I have inserted the recipe for making a *mirepoix*, which is a basic combination that you can use in this and many other recipes. I have also added the recipe for *Duxelles*, which is a simple chopped mushroom mix used to enrich sauces.

BASIC, or MEDIUM, BÉCHAMEL (WHITE SAUCE)
(Makes about 1cup)
In a sauce pan, melt over medium heat

2 Tbs.	**shortening** (butter is best)

Stir in till smooth

2 Tbs.	**flour**

Add, stirring vigorously

1 c.	**milk** or **stock** (preferably heated)
pinch	**salt** and **pepper**, if using just milk

Bring to the simmering point, stirring to prevent lumps from forming. Cook gently for 5 to 10 minutes. You can shorten the time if you are in a hurry, but be sure that the mixture comes to a simmer, so that the flour will be cooked.

If it thickens too much, gradually add a little more milk. This will be your all-purpose sauce. Its uses are endless.

NOTE: You can use slightly soured milk, but be careful. If too soured, add ¼ tsp. baking soda.

BINDING BÉCHAMEL

Follow the above procedure for making a béchamel, but use a ratio of **3: 5½:1** (3 Tbs. shortening: 5½ Tbs. flour: 1 cup liquid) to obtain a binding béchamel. If possible, use a liquid appropriate for your leftovers, e.g. chicken stock for chicken or vegetables. Cook gently till there is no more flour taste. Keep warm till used.

BASIC BROWN SAUCE

The proportions of this sauce are slightly different from those of the basic béchamel, namely **2: 2: 2½** (2 Tbs. shortening: 2 Tbs. flour: 2½ c. liquid). It starts out being quite liquid, but you need to reduce it by letting it simmer an hour or so till you end up with about a cup.

(Makes about 1 cup)

Melt	2 Tbs.	**shortening**
Add and simmer gently		
	½	**carrot**, peeled and chopped
	½	**onion**, chopped
	½ to 1 stalk	**celery**, chopped
	Or ½ to 1 c.	*mirepoix* (see recipe page 12)
Stir in	2 Tbs.	**flour**
When slightly brown, add		
	½ c.	**canned tomatoes** or **tomato sauce**
Stir and add	2 c.	**beef stock** (or microwave 2 c. **water** with 1 **beef bouillon cube**)

Simmer uncovered until the mixture is reduced by half (1 to 1½ hours). It should be smooth and have a nice dark brown color. You can jazz it up with a splash of **red wine** or by adding **Madeira** wine for use with eggs or chicken. Brown sauce is the preferred sauce to use with warmed-up red meats. A delicious enhancement is to add some cooked **mushrooms** or *Duxelles* (see recipe page 12).

BÉCHAMEL-BASED SAUCES

I am always amazed at the versatility of the basic procedure described above. It can be used as a jumping-off point for an array of interesting sauces that will liven up your reheated leftovers. You can enrich it by adding cream or an egg yolk. If you do the latter, gently boil the sauce first, then remove from heat before adding the yolk, otherwise the sauce will curdle. You may need to add some extra liquid depending on how runny you want the sauce. The following recipes, which explain what to add to your basic béchamel sauce, are short-cuts to some classic sauces. Here are some examples.

VELOUTÉ: This is the name given to a béchamel made with veal or chicken stock.

MUSTARD SAUCE: Add a blob (about a Tbs.) of **Dijon mustard** and serve over reheated cauliflower, broccoli, cabbage, Brussels sprouts, etc. The further addition of some chopped unsweetened **pickles**, and some **capers** makes a wonderful sauce to use with reheated slices of ham, tongue, or any smoked pork, especially if you have made the béchamel with the cooking stock of these meats. It can be used with grilled fish, too.

HORSERADISH SAUCE: Add about a Tbs. of creamed **horseradish** and a tsp. of Dijon **mustard**. Use over reheated slices of pot roast or corned beef.

CUCUMBER SAUCE: Peel, remove the seeds, and cut into small cubes a **cucumber**. Simmer them briefly in a small quantity of water just to soften them. Drain, but keep the cooking water, which you will use to make the béchamel. Add **cream** or **milk** to the sauce if necessary. If the sauce is too blah, stir in half a vegetable bouillon cube. Stir in the cucumber cubes. Serve over reheated fish or seafood.

This procedure can also be used with chopped **celery** instead of the cucumber. Add some grated **nutmeg**.

CHEESE SAUCE (Mornay sauce): This is a universal sauce. Just grate some **cheese**, the sharper the better, into the basic béchamel and add some grated **nutmeg**. If it needs a bit more pizzazz, add half a **bouillon cube** and/ or a splash of **white wine**. Its uses are infinite! If using for a gratinée (see page 81) go easy on the cheese and use a little extra liquid. Great over sliced hard-boiled eggs for a meatless dish.

CURRY SAUCE: Simmer some cut-up **onions** in the butter/shortening and stir in about 2 Tbs. **curry** powder before adding the flour and liquid. You can also stir in some cut-up pieces of **apple** with the onion. (See Chapter 19, Curries, page 96.)

SEAFOOD SAUCE: Mash some leftover cooked **shrimp** and add to basic béchamel. Better yet if you can make the béchamel with shrimp or seafood cooking water. You can add a Tbs. of **tomato paste** or a tsp. of **dried tarragon** (not both). Other possible additions: chopped, cooked **oysters**; chopped **anchovies**. Use over pasta or reheated fish.

MUSHROOM SAUCE: Simmer some chopped **onions** in the butter/ shortening with some sliced or chopped **mushrooms** before adding the flour and liquid. This sauce has many uses and is especially good over reheated chicken, steak or beef, and, of course, pasta.

LEMON-FLAVORED BÉCHAMEL (Allemande sauce): Make the béchamel with **chicken broth** (you can use a chicken bouillon cube) combined with a little **milk**. When cooked and smooth, add a little **cream** and an **egg yolk**. Stir in well but don't let it come to the boil. Add a Tbs. **lemon juice**. Good served over warmed-up chicken, veal, or vegetables.

ONION or LEEK SAUCE: Slowly simmer a chopped **onion** or the chopped stem (white part) of one large **leek** in the butter till they are translucent. Finish procedure with the flour and liquid. Add 1 Tbs. finely chopped **parsley**, if desired.

CAPER SAUCE: Make a light béchamel using the stock from **meat** or **ham bones** and a little **white wine** (optional). Add about a Tbs. of **Dijon mustard** and some chopped **sour dill pickles** and **capers**.

SIMPLE CREAMY TOMATO SAUCE: Make a light béchamel, sautéing a little chopped **onion** and **garlic** in the butter before adding the liquid (preferably well-flavored stock). Stir in 1 to 2 Tbs. **tomato paste**. Modify with some **half & half**. Adjust the seasoning, adding **herbs** if desired.

ALFREDO SAUCE: Simmer some chopped **onions** and **garlic** in **olive oil**, rather than butter, before stirring in the flour. Add **half & half** for the liquid. Add some grated **Parmesan** cheese and grated **nutmeg**. You can also add a small splash of **white wine**.

MAKING DISHES with BÉCHAMEL

To preserve the delicate flavor of some leftovers, for example **fish**, **shrimp**, or **veal**, one of the most satisfying ways to recycle them is to incorporate them into a cream sauce, which you can use to fill crêpes, turnovers, puff pastry shells, or simply serve over pasta, toast or fried bread. You can also thicken the béchamel with an **egg yolk** and spread it over your leftovers in a greased ovenproof dish, sprinkle on some **bread crumbs**, dot with **butter**, and put under the broiler for a few minutes, thus converting it into a gratinée.

Please see Chapters 12, 15, and 16 for ideas. You will be starting out with the same basic procedure for making a béchamel, except that in many recipes you will be simmering ingredients, such as onions and/or mushrooms, in the butter before adding the flour and liquid.

MIREPOIX

Mirepoix is the French word for a basic mix of chopped onions, celery, and carrots that you will use time and time again. You can make it on the spot, or you can make up a batch and freeze it for future use. Use it for extra flavor when you start to make a béchamel.

In a heavy-bottomed saucepan, simmer together over low heat

	2 to 4 Tbs.	**butter**, **olive oil**, or **vegetable oil**
Add a ratio of	2 parts	**onions**, finely chopped
	1 part	**celery**, finely chopped
	1 part	**carrots**, peeled and finely chopped

Your choice of butter or oil will depend on your recipe (e.g. butter for fish, olive oil for meats). When the vegetables are wilted and most of the moisture has evaporated, the *mirepoix* is ready. If you want a white mixture, omit the carrots. You might not care for celery, but its flavor is barely noticeable in this treatment, and it adds depth to your sauces.

DUXELLES

This is the French name for a preparation of chopped **mushroom stems** that can be stored and later added to give character to all sorts of dishes where the addition of mushrooms is appropriate. It not only uses up the less desirable parts of mushrooms, it is also a valuable addition to your arsenal.

In a heavy-bottomed saucepan, simmer together over low heat

	2 to 4 Tbs.	**butter, olive oil**, or **vegetable oil**
A ratio of	2 parts	**mushroom stems**, chopped,squeezed dry*
	1 part	**onions**, finely chopped
	1 small clove	**garlic**, whole

Do not let this mixture brown.

When steam stops rising, remove garlic clove and season with

salt and pepper

| Add | 1 tsp. to 1 Tbs. | **parsley**, chopped |
| | ¼ tsp. | **nutmeg**, grated |

If not used immediately, freeze or store in a sealed jar in the fridge for about a week.

* Put them in a paper towel and squeeze out the juice.

BASIC GRAVY

You have probably done a streamlined version of the above many times when you made gravy for roast meat or chicken. After removing the roast from the pan (which must be metal) and placing it over medium heat, you sprinkled a couple of tablespoons of **flour** into the drippings, stirred till there were no more lumps and the mixture turned a mellow brown, and then poured in some **liquid** (wine, stock, milk, slightly soured milk, or even just water), swishing it around and stirring until all was well blended, scraping up any bits stuck to the bottom. You adjusted the seasoning and let it simmer a few minutes before straining it into the gravy boat. What could have been easier?

However, there are many ways to enhance this process, mainly by adding chopped **onions** (or a *mirepoix*, page 12) to the drippings and stewing them a few minutes before adding the flour. Or you can add sliced **mushrooms** (or a *Duxelles*, page 12). You can also add more herbs or jazz up the sauce with cayenne pepper or paprika.

BASIC TOMATO SAUCE

(Makes 4 to 5 cups)

Heat	2 Tbs.	**oil** (preferably olive)
Chop coarsely	1	**carrot**
	½ large	**onion**
	2 cloves	**garlic**
	1 large stalk	**celery**
	1 Tbs.	**parsley** (use stems)
Sprinkle with	2 Tbs.	**flour**

Stir well. Add and bring to simmer

	28 oz. can	**diced tomatoes**
(Optional)	¼ c.	red or white **wine**

Meanwhile, in small bowl, dissolve together

	1 small can	**tomato paste**
	1 c.	**milk**, 2% or whole
Beat in	2 Tbs.	**flour**

Add this mixture slowly to the saucepan contents, beating with a whisk.
Enhance seasoning with **salt**, **pepper**, **herbes de Provence**, or any combination of **oregano**, **basil**, **thyme**, **rosemary**. Go heavy on the **rosemary** if using with lamb.

Bring to a very slow simmer and continue to cook for 1 to 2 hours (the longer the better), stirring occasionally to prevent sticking. Be sure to scrape the bottom. Continue to correct the consistency by adding a little water, stock, or milk if necessary.

This sauce will increase in flavor over a few days spent in your refrigerator.

OTHER SAUCES, NOT BÉCHAMEL-BASED

Among the encyclopedic collection of possible sauces, here are a few more that are easy to make and can be considered essential for dressing up freshly cooked or leftover food. The following examples are streamlined versions of classic sauces.

HOLLANDAISE SAUCE

Classic method

(Makes about 1 cup)

In small metal bowl or the top of a double boiler, combine

2	**egg yolks**
3 Tbs.	**lemon juice**
1 stick (4 oz.)	**butter**, cut in medium-large pieces
pinch	**salt**, if butter is unsalted

Place container over, not in, a saucepan of simmering water. Beat with a whisk until the butter has melted. Keep beating vigorously, scraping the sides, until the sauce has stiffened to desired texture. Be careful not to cook it too long, as it will become grainy. Pour into serving dish immediately. Serve warm or at room temperature.

Blender method

(Makes about ¾ cup)

Melt 1 stick (4 oz.) **butter**

Combine in blender

3	**egg yolks**
1 to 2 Tbs.	**lemon juice**
pinch	**salt**

On low speed, mix the yolks and lemon juice. Very slowly dribble in the melted butter. Keep scraping the mixture from the sides. Sauce is ready when all the butter is absorbed. Serve warm or at room temperature.

MOUSSELINE SAUCE

This sauce is a lighter, creamier version of hollandaise sauce. It is good with fish and vegetables, such as asparagus, artichokes, spinach, broccoli, cauliflower. Serve at room temperature.

Follow the directions for Classic or Blender Hollandaise above. When the sauce is cool, whip until stiff ¼ c. **whipping cream** and incorporate it into the sauce. Makes about 1½ cups.

CHIFFON SAUCE

Perhaps you are wondering what to do with those egg whites left over from the hollandaise. You can whip one or two of them till stiff with a pinch of salt and fold them into the cooled hollandaise sauce. This will result in a lighter and frothier hollandaise. I like it with asparagus and artichokes.

Because this sauce uses uncooked egg whites, it should be used up immediately and not stored. Serve at room temperature.

BÉARNAISE SAUCE

This sauce is similar to hollandaise but uses **vinegar** instead of lemon. **Tarragon**, dried or fresh, is also called for. It is recommended for use with grilled meats or fish.

Classic Method

(Makes about 1 cup)

In small metal bowl or the top of a double boiler combine

2	**egg yolks**
2 Tbs.	**red wine vinegar**
1 stick (4 oz.)	**butter**, cut in medium-large pieces
pinch	**salt**, if butter unsalted
1 Tbs.	**shallot** or **onion**, minced
1 tsp.	**tarragon**, dried or chopped fresh

Place bowl over, not in, a saucepan of simmering water. Beat with a whisk until the butter has melted. Keep beating vigorously, scraping the sides, until the sauce has stiffened to desired texture. Be careful not to cook it too long, as it will become grainy. Pour into serving dish immediately to stop the cooking process.

I often use the above method with **whole eggs** instead of just the yolks. This method will make a paler sauce and should be removed from the heat while still fairly runny, or it will become lumpy. Be sure to beat it vigorously to give it a creamy texture.

Blender Method

(Makes about ¾ cup)

Melt	1 stick (4 oz.)	**butter**
Combine in blender		
	3	**egg yolks**
	1 to 2 Tbs.	**red wine vinegar**
	pinch	**salt**
	1 Tbs.	**shallot** or **onion**, minced
	1 tsp.	**tarragon**, dried

On low speed, mix the blender ingredients. Very slowly dribble in the melted butter. Keep scraping the mixture from the sides. Sauce is ready when all the butter is absorbed.

CHAPTER 3: HORS D'OEUVRE

All sorts of odds and ends can be used for dips and canapés. For dips, you will be blending them in with some fresh ingredients. For canapés, they will have picked up extra flavor since their debut. Here are a few suggestions to get you started. Measurements are inexact, as they depend on the quantity and contents of your leftovers.

DIPS

SPINACH is a favorite. Chop leftover cooked spinach very fine. Mix it with some **sour cream**, minced **onions** or **chives**, and/or cooked **mushrooms**, and a dash of **nutmeg**. Optional: add a little chopped **garlic** and/or **basil**. Serve with potato chips.

COOKED LENTILS or BEANS can be puréed in a blender with **olive oil**, chopped **onions**, chopped **garlic**, a few pitted **olives**, and **herbs** or seasoning of your choice. If too bland, add a drop or two of **lemon juice**, **vinegar**, **red wine**, or **hot sauce**. Sprinkle with **grated cheese**, if desired. Serve with corn chips.

Another version of a **LENTIL or BEAN** dip is to add minced **ham** to the above recipe. Pulse it first in a food processor, and then add the other ingredients. Dribble in the **oil** and liquid ingredients (not lemon juice; substitute **white wine**). Rosemary seasoning is particularly good. Serve with potato chips.

A version of **BABA GHANOUSH** can be made with peeled, cooked **eggplant**. Mix it with some **tahini**, and, depending on the makeup of your leftovers, add chopped **garlic**, **olive oil**, and **lemon juice**. Purée in blender and serve sprinkled with chopped parsley with mini pita bread.

Another **COOKED EGGPLANT** dip can be made from a leftover **eggplant casserole**, preferably made with peeled eggplant. Chances are it will contain **tomatoes**, **onions**, **garlic**, maybe **olives**, and assorted **herbs**. If necessary, moisten with a little **red wine**, **olive oil**, and/or **balsamic vinegar**. Add some diced **tomatoes** if there are none in the leftovers. Purée in blender and serve topped with a sprinkling of **grated cheese** and a sprig of **basil** or **rosemary**. Good with mini pita bread or crisp toast rounds.

CANAPÉS

By reducing the size, you can adapt many of the procedures described in this manual to tasty canapés or nibblies. Think quiches (see page 51) and turnovers (see page 79), both of which need pastry dough filled with the mixtures you have used for croquettes, mousses, timbales, etc. Below I have listed some suggested fillings. Some chunky leftovers can be transformed by wrapping bacon around them and grilling, or they can be put on mini-skewers and grilled. Here are a few suggestions.

HOT CANAPÉS

QUICHES or TARTLETS

Roll out regular pie pastry dough. Cut into small rounds and place in tartlet molds. Fill with any of the fillings suggested below and bake at **400° F** for **15 to 20 minutes**.

TURNOVERS

Roll out pie or biscuit dough and cut into small triangles. Pile a little filling in center, wet the borders of the dough, fold over and press edges to seal. Bake in **400° F** oven for about **20 minutes**.

SUGGESTED FILLINGS for MINI-QUICHES or TURNOVERS

You are limited by only your leftover supply and your imagination. Here are some that work well.

- ❖ Creamed **mushrooms**
- ❖ Any croquette mix with **chicken, shrimp,** or **crabmeat**
- ❖ Any chicken or **seafood salad mix** (no dressing)
- ❖ **Curried mixes** of chicken or shrimp
- ❖ Chopped **sausages** with touch of **mustard**

SKEWERS

You can combine leftover chunks of **meat, chicken, turkey,** or **shrimp** on mini skewers with small pieces of **onion, dried fruit, red** or **yellow pepper,**

melon, **olives**, etc. **Lamb** chunks are good with **eggplant**, **olives**, and **onion** pieces. Coat lightly with olive oil and grill 8 to 10 minutes, turning once or twice. Serve with a mustard or cocktail sauce.

BACON-WRAPPED CANAPÉS

Cooked **shrimp**, **scallops**, **chicken chunks**, **chicken livers** can be wrapped in partially-cooked **bacon**, secured with a toothpick, and grilled till the bacon is cooked.

MINI-CROQUETTES

Use the recipes in Chapter 14 (see page 73) for croquettes, only make them smaller. Make sure the bread crumb coating is thick and seals in the filling before deep frying.

COLD CANAPÉS

Open-faced mini-sandwiches are a good way to use up semi-stale bread, as its stiffness will prevent the canapé from collapsing. Make a salad mix of your leftovers with homemade mayonnaise (see page 33). For an extra flourish, you can coat the sandwich with a layer of aspic (see page 41) and refrigerate immediately. Be sure to decorate the top of the sandwiches with a sprig of parsley, tarragon, or julienned tomato or ham strips. You can dust them with chopped hard-boiled egg yolks or perch a caper or pickle slice on top. Here are a few suggestions.

SHRIMP & AVOCADO

Chop some cooked **shrimp** and marinate in a mixture of **lime juice**, minced **onions**, and **cilantro**. Meanwhile mash an **avocado** with some minced **garlic** and **salsa**.
Spread the avocado mix on toasted rounds of **white bread**. Top with the drained marinated shrimp. Garnish with a sprig of cilantro.

HAM WRAPS

Strips of thin slices of **ham** can be wrapped around pieces of cooked vegetables such as **asparagus**, **snow peas**, or **green string beans**. Bundle the vegetable pieces according to how thin they are and baste the center area with a thin coat of homemade mayonnaise. Fasten a strip of ham around them with a toothpick. A tiny blob of mayo topped with a mini-leaf of parsley is a nice garnish.

Leftover **scallops** can also be wrapped with ham slices. Add a little chopped **cilantro** to the mayonnaise.

LIVER PÂTÉ

What a delicious way to use those chicken or duck livers and hearts that came in the giblet package tucked inside the bird! Or if, like us, you love veal liver and cooked a bit too much, you can convert that, too.

Sauté some chopped **onions** and a little **garlic** in **olive oil**. If the chicken livers and hearts are raw, chop and sauté them with the onions. (Don't use the gizzards; save them for the stock pot.) If they are cooked, just chop them and add after cooking the onion/garlic mix. Put the liver mixture in a blender with pinch of **sage** and chopped **parsley** and a small dash of **red wine** or **port**. Season carefully with salt and pepper. Pulse briefly, taking care that the mixture doesn't become liquid. Taste and adjust the seasoning. Chill for a few hours or overnight to stiffen it up.

Spread on slightly stale **white bread** slices or toast rounds. Top with a small **pickle** slice or a **caper**.

MOCK PÂTÉ de FOIE GRAS

This pâté is truly heavenly. You will almost believe you are savoring the real thing. It is a slight elaboration on the liver pâté recipe above. The following one is for a pound of chicken livers, so you may have to go and buy some to add to your bird's liver. Don't use the heart for this recipe: liver only.

From your arsenal   **A blender**

Remove any sinews, fat, or dark spots, but leave intact.

1 lb	**raw chicken** or **duck livers**

Put them in a bowl, cover with **milk**

Let them soak about an hour to remove any bitter taste. Drain them and discard the milk.

Melt in skillet till foaming

2 Tbs.	**unsalted butter**

Add the livers and sauté over medium-high heat.

Cook them until all the liquid is evaporated and the livers are browned but still a bit pink in the middle (about 10 minutes).

Scrape into a **blender**.

Add to blender	⅓ c.	**heavy cream**
	6 Tbs. (3 oz.)	**unsalted butter**, melted
	2 to 3 Tbs.	**port** or **brandy**
	pinch	**salt** and **pepper** (freshly ground if possible. Green pepper is also good.)

Go fairly strong on the seasonings to compensate for the loss of flavor when chilled.

Purée this mixture, starting slowly and working up to high speed. You will need to stop often to scrape the sides. Keep puréeing at top speed until the mixture is as smooth as velvet.

Pour into a terrine or bowl, cover tightly (not with aluminum foil) and refrigerate for several hours or overnight, if possible. The pâté will harden and you will be able to make slices to put on thin slices of toasted white bread.

If you wish to keep the pâté for longer than overnight, cover it with melted chicken or duck fat.

———————————

CHAPTER 4: SOUPS

These can be hot or cold, depending on the season. Made a day ahead of time, they taste better. Your stand-by is a basic stock, whether it is one you have made or one from a can or bouillon cubes. Amazing results can come from combining leftovers in a blender. The combinations are endless.

From your arsenal	**A blender** **Basic stock** (see recipe below) *Or* **bouillon cubes** **Roux** (see recipe below)

Almost any kind of leftover can be puréed in a blender. (Corn is great.) If it is dry, add a little **water, milk, half & half, heavy cream**, or **sour cream**. Add **stock** (home made or from a can) or a **bouillon cube** dissolved in hot water.

Add **curry** or any other **spice or herb**, if desired.

BASIC STOCK

Put in a large pot	2 Tbs.	**oil** (olive or canola)
	¼ c. each	**carrots, celery, onions**, chopped (or some *mirepoix*)
	1 Tbs. each	**garlic, parsley stems**, chopped

Cover pot and simmer these ingredients gently over low heat till soft and only slightly browned.

Add		**a chicken or turkey carcass** (don't forget drippings, skin, gravy) *Or* **bones** from **chicken breasts** *Or* **meat bones** and **scraps** *Or* **fish bones** or **shrimp shells** **spices** (pepper corns, bay leaves, herbes de Provence, etc.)
	1 tsp. each	**salt** and **pepper**

Fill pot with **water** and cover. Simmer for 2 to 3 hours. (A pressure cooker will speed up the process.) Drain through a colander into a large bowl. Let the stock cool and skim off the fat if you wish to use it immediately. If you wish to refrigerate it, leave the fat, as it will help in preservation.

NOTE: A **ham bone** makes a delicious and versatile stock. Cover it with water, add some chopped **veggies**, cooked or raw, bring to a boil, skim off any scum, and simmer for 2 to 3 hours. Or you can use the stock to cook some chopped veggies with and then purée with a little **milk** or **half & half**. Be careful when puréeing; pulse it in batches so it doesn't splash over.

Use stock made with a ham bone to cook **split peas** (follow directions on the package). Purée in blender and add a little **milk** or **half & half**.

VEGETARIAN STOCK

You can make a vegetarian stock by simply omitting the meat. **Tomatoes** (canned or fresh) are a good addition, along with chopped leftover **vegetables** and a vegetable or herb **bouillon cube**.

NOTE: This stock can be converted into a delicious puréed vegetable soup by processing it in the blender. Add **milk** or **half & half** for extra richness.

WARNING! Don't use much salt, as you will be adjusting the taste according to the leftovers you are adding. Remember that bouillon cubes are very salty!

TIP: When you boil or steam some vegetables, don't throw out the **cooking water**. It will keep for several days in the fridge. Use it with, or instead of, stock in many recipes. But remember, it, too, will be salty. Good cooking water to preserve: **green beans**, **corn**, **carrots**, **peas**, **onions**, **potatoes**. Forget about cauliflower or any of the cabbage family.

The same goes for water used to cook **shrimp**, **clams**, **mussels**, or other **seafood**.

ROUX-BASED STOCK

To make a tastier soup and if you would like to thicken the soup, you can start with a roux and add stock mixed with your chopped leftovers.

In a sauce pan melt

	2 Tbs.	**shortening** (butter or margarine)
Stir in	2 Tbs.	**flour**

Cook slowly till flour is golden to dark brown. This is your roux.

Add and stir	2 to 4 c.	**stock**
Add	1 c.	**leftovers**, chopped

Simmer about **1 hour** to blend the flavors. Drain through a colander.

VARIATION: Use the **outside leaves of iceberg**, **romaine**, or **leaf lettuce**. Shred them, and cook them gently in the shortening before adding the flour and stock. Use a strong beef or chicken bouillon or stock.

NOTE: The tough, outside leaves of lettuce are also excellent when cut up and cooked with spinach leaves.

———————

HOT SOUPS

BARLEY SOUP

This soup is especially good to use up pieces of cooked **lamb**. Perhaps you have already cooked barley as a side dish for the lamb (a lovely combination), in which case you only need to add it to stock made with lamb bones and scraps, and add cut up pieces of lamb.

If you need to cook the **barley,** follow the directions on the package. The general ratio is one part barley to three parts liquid. It needs to simmer about **45 minutes**. Cook it in stock for added flavor, or use a bouillon cube.

Follow the recipe on page above to make a **roux-based stock**. Add the **lamb scraps** to the roux and simmer briefly before adding the stock. Add the barley, adjust the seasoning, and simmer for about **1½ hours** to blend the flavors.

BEEF SOUP with POTATOES

If you have leftover beef and mashed or baked potatoes, you can make this hearty soup and serve it with a salad as a light lunch.

(Serves about 6)

Cut into small cubes

2 to 3 c.	**cooked beef**

If you are using leftover steak or roast beef, sauté the cubes briefly in oil till lightly browned. Set aside.

In a large pot, heat

2 Tbs.	**olive** or **canola oil**

Add and sauté lightly

½ c. each	**carrots, onions, celery**, chopped

When these are wilted, add

2 Tbs. each	**garlic** and **parsley stems**, chopped
(Optional) Add 1 c.	**mushrooms**, sliced

Cook for about **5 minutes**. Add and stir in the reserved meat cubes.

Add

1	**bay leaf**
1 to 2 c.	**beef stock** (use beef bouillon cubes if you like)
½ to 1 c.	**mashed potatoes**
	Or **riced* baked or boiled potatoes**

Stir this mixture well.

Add 5 to 6 c. more **beef stock**

Mix well, adjust the seasoning, and simmer for about **an hour**. You can add a splash of 1 to 2 Tbs. **red wine** to jazz it up, or you can add 1 to 2 Tbs. **cream** for a more soothing product.

NOTE: For an extra hearty meal, try adding some cooked egg noodles before serving.

* If you don't have a ricer, a.k.a. food mill (a contraption with a rotating handle that pushes soft food through a disk with holes), force the potato flesh with the back of a spoon through a large sieve or colander.

CREAM of CHICKEN and ASPARAGUS SOUP
(Serves about 6)

Cut into small cubes and set aside

| | 1 to 1½ c. | **cooked chicken** |

In a large pot, heat

| | 2 Tbs. | **olive oil** |
| | 2 Tbs. | **butter** |

Add and simmer till wilted

	1	**onion**, large, chopped
	Or 1	**leek**, the white part only, slivered
	1 Tbs.	**celery**, minced
Sprinkle with	1 Tbs.	**flour**
Stir and add	6 c.	**chicken stock**
Add	1 Tbs.	**dried tarragon**
	Or 2 Tbs.	**fresh tarragon**

Simmer for about **30 minutes**.

| Add | 1 c. | **asparagus**, cooked, cut in small pieces |

Transfer to blender in batches and pulse till puréed. If too stringy, put through a strainer. Put puréed mixture back in the pot to reheat.

Adjust flavor by adding **chicken bouillon cubes** if necessary.
Adjust the thickness by adding **milk** or **heavy cream**.
Reheat, but do not bring to a boil.

NOTE: This soup can be served chilled. Garnish with **croutons, chopped chives**, or a **tarragon sprig**.

NOTE: If you find that your soup is turning out too runny, you can resort to **cornstarch**, but you must be sure that it comes to the boil. Dissolve 1 to 2 Tbs. cornstarch in some **cold liquid** (milk, stock, etc.) and add it to the simmering soup.

TURKEY SOUP

Here is one way to honor the last days of the holiday turkey.

For the STOCK

Put in a large pot		**a turkey carcass**
	1	**onion**, chopped
	1 to 2 stalks	**celery**, chopped
	1 large or 2 small	**carrots**, chopped
	2 to 3	**garlic cloves** in their skin
	¼ c.	**parsley stems**, chopped
	2 to 3	**bay leaves**
	1 sprig	**rosemary**
	¼ tsp.	**ground sage**
		salt and **pepper** to taste

Cover with cold water and bring to the boil, skimming off the scum as it rises.

Simmer for about **3 hours**, adding water if necessary. From time to time, you can mush the ingredients around to extract the most goodness from them.

Remove from heat and let cool to lukewarm. Pour into a colander placed over a large bowl and allow to drain well.

Chill the stock and scrape the fat off the top if you plan to use the stock right away. Otherwise leave the fat to help preserve it.

For the SOUP

(Serves 4 to 5)

In a large saucepan, melt		
	2 Tbs.	**butter**
Add and simmer till wilted		
	1	**carrot**, sliced thin
	½ large	**onion**, sliced thin
	1 c.	**outer lettuce leaves**, shredded
Sprinkle with	1 to 2 tsp.	**flour**
Add	4 to 5 c.	**stock**

Bring to a gentle boil and simmer about **20 minutes**.
Serve with **croutons** and grated **Parmesan** cheese.

———————

BORSCHCH*

This Russian soup comes in many variations and is a great way to use up extra cooked beef. Although some of the ingredients can be improvised, the basic two, cabbage and beets, remain. If you don't have beef stock on hand, use bouillon cubes. Remember, they are very salty. This is a hearty soup, good for a chilly, winter supper.

* If you are wondering about the spelling of borschch, it is the most accurate rendering of the Russian sound Щ (shcha), as in БОРЩ.

(Serves about 6)

Heat in large saucepan

	2 Tbs.	**olive oil**
Sauté till wilted	1	**onion**, chopped
	4 to 5 cloves	**garlic**, chopped
	½ stalk	**celery**, minced
(Optional)	½ bulb	**fennel**, chopped
Add	2 c.	**red or green cabbage**, shredded
	2 c.	**beets**, peeled and cut into small cubes

Simmer until cabbage is wilted. Season with **salt** and **pepper**.

Mix together	2 Tbs.	**tomato paste**
	2 Tbs.	**red wine vinegar**

Add to cabbage/beet mixture.

Add	1 to 2 c.	**cooked beef**, diced
	6 c.	**beef stock** (or equivalent made with bouillon cubes)
	1 large	**bay leaf**

Stir until well mixed. Cover and simmer over low heat for about an hour. If you like, you can add for the last 15 minutes

	1 c.	**potatoes**, peeled, cut into small cubes

Serve piping hot with a blob of **sour cream** and chopped **chives** sprinkled on top.

If you have not added potatoes to the soup, serve hot, **boiled potatoes** on the side. Or you can just serve the soup with slices of the darkest bread you can find.

VARIATION: In Russia, borschch is sometimes made with kvass, a beer-like brew made from black bread or other ingredients. If you like adventure, you could substitute some **dark ale** for part of the beef stock.

NOTE: When you buy fresh beets, look for a bunch with nice, green leaves. You can use them to make a delicious side dish. Remove the red stem and veins from the leaves and cook about 10 minutes in a little water, a little longer than you would fresh spinach. Drain, chop, and serve with butter or sour cream.

EGG DROP SOUP

(Serves 4 to 5)

This is an easy way to use up scraps of chicken, turkey, or pork. If possible, cut the meat scraps into neat strips. You can also add a little leftover vegetable like spinach or carrots.

Bring to a boil	about 5 c.	**chicken stock** (if not available, use bouillon cubes)
Add	1 tsp.	**grated ginger**

Simmer for a few minutes.

Beat lightly and add

	2	**eggs**

Stir the eggs gently for about 30 seconds.

Add	½ c.	**cooked meat**, shredded
	¼ c.	**cooked vegetables**, shredded

Stir for another 30 seconds and serve.

SUGGESTED COMBINATIONS for SOUPS

- ❖ **Spinach** with **cream**. Add a little grated nutmeg.
- ❖ **Potatoes** with **onions, carrots, celery**
- ❖ **Corn** and **chicken** (keep the chicken in chunks)
- ❖ **Corn** and **shrimp**. Use shrimp stock with leftover shrimp.
- ❖ **Fish chowder**. Use fish stock with cooked fish pieces, corn, or potatoes.
- ❖ **Cauliflower** and **ham chunks**. Purée the cauliflower with cream, milk, or stock and add the ham pieces.
- ❖ **Broccoli** with **cheese**. Make cream of broccoli by puréeing

cooked broccoli and adding milk and/or half and half. Top with small cheese chunks.

❖ **Beef** chunks with **vegetables, rice** in a beef stock
❖ **Chicken** chunks with **rice** or **pasta** in chicken stock
❖ **Dried peas** or **beans** cooked in **ham stock**

COLD SOUPS

COLD ZUCCHINI or VEGETABLE CURRIED SOUP
(Serves 4)

Put aside	¼ c.	**vegetables**, cooked, julienned

In a saucepan, combine

	2 c.	**vegetables (zucchini, carrots, broccoli**, etc.), cooked, chopped
	½ c.	**onion**, chopped
	1 to 2 tsp.	**curry** powder

Mix well and add

2 c. combined **chicken stock, milk, half & half,** or **heavy cream**

Simmer for 45 minutes. Adjust the seasoning and thickness (the soup will thicken when cold). Let cool a bit.

Purée this mixture in a blender, taking care not to let it spurt over. You may have to do this in two batches. Pour into a bowl and add the reserved vegetable strips.

Refrigerate until thoroughly chilled and serve topped with **chopped chives**.

COLD BANANA CREAM SOUP with CURRY

This sounds like a strange combination, but it is very good. You can also serve it hot. It makes an excellent starter course and is an elegant funeral for those mushy bananas.

(Serves 4 to 5)

Dissolve together

2	**vegetable** or **chicken bouillon cubes**
4 c.	**hot water**
Or 4 c.	**vegetable** or **chicken stock**

Set aside.

In a large saucepan, over low heat melt

3 Tbs.	**butter**

Add and stir well

3 Tbs.	**flour**

Do not let the mixture brown.
While stirring, add

½ c.	**milk**, or a combination of **milk** and **half & half**

Add the reserved bouillon or stock.
Bring to a simmer and add

2 medium	**bananas**, sliced

Simmer for a few minutes.

Put batches into blender and purée, starting on low to prevent spilling over. Return to saucepan and bring to a simmer.

In a small bowl, mix

1 to 2 tsp.	**curry** powder
¼ c.	**cream**

(Optional, if soup is too liquid)

1 Tbs.	**cornstarch**

Add this mixture to the simmering soup and stir in well. Watch out that it doesn't foam over. Adjust the seasoning with salt and pepper and simmer a few more minutes to make sure the cornstarch is cooked. Stir to prevent foaming.

Serve topped with **thin slices of banana** and finely chopped **chives**.

CHAPTER 5: SALAD DRESSINGS & SALADS

All sorts of odds and ends can be combined to make a delicious salad. You be the creative chef. What *is* important, though, is the dressing. Here are two recipes, one for homemade **mayonnaise**, which should be on hand at all times, the only exception being Hellman's Original Mayonnaise or some other brand that has minimum sugar content. The other recipe is a simple one for **vinaigrette** (**Balsamic** or **plain**), which I keep in a bottle so I don't have to mix it each time.

SALAD DRESSINGS

HOMEMADE MAYONNAISE

This needs to be a constant in your fridge, as its wonderful flavor will boost the blandness of any leftover. The ingredients should be as cold as possible, as the processing will warm them up.

(Makes about 1½ cups)

You will need		**a blender**
Measure	1 c.	**vegetable oil** (not olive)
Put in blender	1	**egg**
	1 tsp.	**mustard**, Dijon style
	1 tsp.	**salt**
	pinch	**pepper**
	1 Tbs.	**lemon juice**
	1 Tbs.	**white wine vinegar**
	3 Tbs.	**of the oil**

Process at top speed for about 15 seconds.

Dribble the rest of the oil, *very* slowly, into the center of the mix while continuing to process at top speed. If it becomes too stiff, stop the process and scrape the sides before continuing. If it seems too soft, don't worry; it will stiffen up in the fridge.* You can add a spoonful of olive oil at the end if you like that flavor.

Depending on your usage, you can make 2 to 3 batches at a time, as this mayonnaise keeps a long time in the fridge. You can divide it up and keep another jar or two with your mayo mixed with other seasonings, e.g. **crushed garlic**, **herbs**, **extra lemon juice**, etc.

* However, if it turns to soup, which it might do on a hot day or if you have added the oil too quickly, put it aside and start all over again with a new batch. When you have completed the second batch, keep processing and add your runny mix by teaspoonfuls. You will end up with a double batch, which you might have intended anyway!

NOTE: This tasty mayonnaise can be used as an emergency quick cold sauce. For example, mix it with a little **water** and **lemon juice**, add a pinch of dried **tarragon**, and serve it over cooled asparagus.

Or dilute it with a little water and **vinegar** and pour it over warm, sliced potatoes.

Or mix it with a little **vinaigrette** (balsamic or otherwise, see below) and use it as a dip for artichokes or over asparagus.

BALSAMIC or PLAIN VINAIGRETTE

Fill a bottle	2/5 full with	**vegetable oil** (preferably canola)
	2/5 full with	**olive oil**
	1/5 full with	**red wine vinegar**
Add	2 tsp.	**Dijon mustard**
	¼ tsp.	**pepper**
	2 tsp.	**salt**
	2 tsp.	**balsamic vinegar**
(Optional, for an extra zip)		a few drops of **lemon juice**

Shake well. This will keep for weeks in your cupboard. No need to refrigerate.

For **plain vinaigrette**, just omit the balsamic vinegar. Increase the lemon juice to 1 Tbs.

As you use up the bottle, you might need to keep adding a little olive or vegetable oil so the dressing doesn't become too sharp.

SUGGESTIONS

This dressing is great with cooked **green beans**, combined with **hard-boiled eggs** and **chopped onions** and a little **garlic**.

It's also good on cooked, warm, cut-up **potatoes**. But dribble a little olive oil over them first.

SALADS

Of the infinite array of salads you can invent using cooked food, here are a few of my favorites.

LENTIL SALAD

The procedure for this salad is infinitely expandable, depending on your supply of leftovers. You can keep it very simple, using for example only some cut-up fresh tomatoes and basil, thus not distracting from the earthy lentil flavor. Or you can combine as many of your leftovers as you can get away with! Be careful not to incorporate ingredients with conflicting tastes.

(Serves 4 to 5)

Put in bowl	2 c.	**cooked lentils**
Add	2	**scallions**, chopped
	1 stalk	**celery**, chopped
	1 clove	**garlic**, minced
	2 Tbs.	**parsley**, chopped
	1 tsp.	**dried herbs** (oregano, thyme, herbes de Provence, etc.)
(Optional)	¼ c.	**tomatoes**, diced, canned or fresh
(Optional)	¼ c.	**ham**, diced
(Optional)	¼ c.	**cooked meat** or **chicken**, chopped
Mix gently and add		
	2 Tbs.	**homemade vinaigrette** (see page 34)

Mix all this together carefully so as not to mash the lentils. Your ingredients will vary according to the contents of the leftover lentil dish. Cut-up cooked **carrots**, **green beans**, **spinach**, **zucchini** are all welcome additions. Adjust the amount of vinaigrette accordingly. Serve at room temperature.

VARIATION: You can use this procedure also with cooked **garbanzos** (chick peas) or other leftover cooked **dried beans** (not with Boston baked beans; they're too sweet!).

RICE COMBINATION SALAD
(Serves 4)

Mix in large bowl

1 c.	**leftover meat, ham, chicken,** or **seafood** cut into julienned strips
2	**scallions,** chopped
Or ¼	**Bermuda onion,** chopped
1 Tbs.	**fresh herbs** or **mint,** chopped
1 clove	**garlic,** minced
¼ c.	**vinaigrette,** balsamic or plain

In another bowl mix together

2 c.	**cooked rice**
2 to 3 Tbs.	**olive oil**

Add rice to ingredients in large bowl and mix gently. Add more dressing if needed and correct the seasoning.

CAULIFLOWER SALAD

Cauliflower happens to be a favorite in our family. The trick is to boil it until it is only just soft, about 6 to 8 minutes for a whole cauliflower or 3 to 5 minutes for florets. After you have enjoyed it for dinner, say, with a lemon sauce or with breadcrumbs and butter spread on top and browned under the broiler, you can give it a whole new life served cold in this simple combination.

In a salad bowl, mix

2 to 3 Tbs.	**mayonnaise**
1 to 2 tsp.	**lemon juice** or **vinaigrette,** or a combination of both

Chop and add   1 Tbs. each   **parsley** and **scallions**
Chop into large chunks

1 to 2	**hard-boiled eggs**

Stir them gently into the mayo mix.
Add and mix gently

2 c.	**leftover cauliflower**

NOTE: Chopped fresh **tomatoes** are a welcome addition in this recipe as in many other salad recipes.

POTATO SALAD

(Serves 4)

Warm 2 minutes in microwave on **power 5**

	6	**boiled or steamed potatoes** (better if skin is left on. Don't use baked ones.)
Have ready	¼ to ⅓ c.	**olive oil**

Slice the potatoes and put in bowl. Pour on olive oil and mix gently so as not to break the potato slices.

Simmer together gently for a few minutes until wilted and set aside

	2 Tbs.	**olive oil**
	1	**yellow or sweet onion**, sliced thin
	Or 5	**scallions**, chopped

In a small bowl, mix together

	¼ c.	**vinaigrette**
	1 Tbs.	**mayonnaise**

Add to potatoes along with the sliced, cooked onions. Mix again very gently.

Serve warm, or let sit a while at room temperature.

STUFFED TOMATOES

(Serves 6)

Have ready	6 large	**tomatoes**

Cut off top of each tomato, put it aside, and scoop out the insides. (Preserve the insides for use in sauces, soups, or stews.) Sprinkle a little salt into the hollows and turn upside down on a paper towel for a few minutes.

Meanwhile, mix together

	¼ to ½ c.	**mayonnaise**
	1 tsp.	**herbs** (parsley, basil, tarragon, cilantro, etc.)
	½	**sweet onion**, chopped
	Or 2 to 3	**scallions**, chopped
(Optional)	1 clove	**garlic**, minced

1½ to 2 c.	**leftover fish**, **seafood**, **chicken**, **meat**, **ham** and/or **vegetables**, chopped

Fill the tomato cases with the mixture, put the tops back on, and place on a lettuce leaf.

NOTE: Remember, it's the quality of the mayonnaise that *makes* this simple dish.

GREEN BEAN SALAD

We eat a lot of green beans and enjoy them even more the next day in salad. There are many possible combinations. Here is an old stand-by.

(Serves 4)

In a bowl, mix	1 to 2 c.	**cooked string beans**
	1 to 2	**scallions**, chopped
	Or 1	**shallot**, chopped
	1 clove	**garlic**, minced
	1 Tbs.	**parsley**, chopped

Dribble in enough **balsamic or basic vinaigrette** to coat the beans well. You can add a chopped **tomato** if you like, and/or a chopped **hard-boiled egg**, but the plain bean salad is easier to use as a side dish.

TIP for COOKING GREEN BEANS

Bring enough salted water to cover the beans to a rolling boil. Add beans and boil uncovered for **7 minutes** in order to cook the starch. They should still be a little crunchy, but should not be hard. If you still taste starch, cook another 1 to 2 minutes.

The classic French way is to boil them uncovered in lots of water. I prefer to use only enough water to barely cover them. That way I have a manageable amount of bean stock left over for other uses. Suit yourself. Either way, unless they are very young and tender, they need *7 minutes* to cook. Run them briefly under cold water to stop the cooking process and preserve the bright green color.

BEETS with HARD-BOILED EGGS

Beets are a classic addition to a plate of crudités (even though they are cooked, not raw). Cut the **cooked beets** into thin slices or strips. Combine with a chopped **hard-boiled egg** or two, some chopped **onions** or **chives** and **parsley**. Mix with some **vinaigrette** to which you may add a Tbs. of **mayonnaise** if you like. Add this combination to a salad of mixed greens, throw in a few chopped walnuts, and you almost have a meal in itself.

TIP for COOKING HARD-BOILED EGGS

Place eggs in cold water in a sauce pan. Bring to boil. Turn off heat, cover, and let sit for **ten minutes**. Immerse in cold water to stop the cooking process. Refrigerate as soon as cool. Use them up soon, as they will not keep for more than about three days. (See Chapter 8, Eggs, page 49, for a quick dish to rescue critical hard-boiled eggs.)

CUCUMBER SALAD

The reason this salad is listed is that it is a wonderful accompaniment to many of the dishes you will have made with your leftovers. I first encountered it at a Swedish smorgasbord (buffet) where it was offered with an array of fish and seafood dishes. But because of its crispness and relatively neutral taste, it goes well with almost any dish for which tomatoes are not appropriate.

Although chopped dill is the classic herb to use, you can vary the herbs and dressing according to the main dish.
(Serves about 4)

Peel and cut in half lengthwise
2 large   **cucumbers**

Scoop out and throw away the seeds, unless they are tiny. Slice *very* thin. You may need a special grater for this. Forget about a food processor; the slices are much too thick. Put slices in a plastic (not metal) colander, sprinkle with **salt**, and let drain for several hours. They should emerge from this process very limp. Mix the cucumber slices with any of the following dressings and herbs.

- ❖ Plain **vinaigrette** (see page 34)
- ❖ Vinaigrette with some chopped fresh **dill**. This is the classic dressing.

❖ **Yogurt** or **sour cream** with **dill**. Another classic.
❖ **Vinaigrette** with a pinch of **tarragon** (for use with fish or seafood) or **parsley**

Go light on the dressing, as the cucumbers will continue to render their water. Avoid mayonnaise for fear of overwhelming the delicate cucumber taste. Chill before serving.

CHAPTER 6: ASPICS (GELÉES)

"Aspic" is not exactly a household word any more, yet food "*en gelée*" is not unusual in French cuisine. Aspics are marvelously refreshing in summer and make a decorative platter or plate. They are also amazingly simple to make.

From your arsenal

Knox unflavored gelatin
Bouillon cubes (beef, chicken, fish, or vegetable)
Or chicken, beef, or fish **stock**
Or canned **broth**
Hard-boiled eggs, sliced
Sprigs of **parsley** or other fresh **herbs**
A mold or **molds** (can be ramekins, a flat-bottomed Pyrex dish, or even a shallow bowl)

GENERAL TECHNIQUE for ASPIC

(Serves 4)

Soak in a little cold water or white wine to soften it

1 envelope   **unflavored gelatin**

Boil   1 cup   **water, stock,** or **broth** (if water, add a bouillon cube)

Add softened gelatin to the hot stock or bouillon. Let cool to lukewarm.

Pour a little on bottom of the mold(s). You can use a glass pie dish or individual ramekins. Let set a few minutes.

Make a decorative arrangement of **sliced hard-boiled eggs** (slip a sprig of **parsley** or other fresh herb under the center slice) on top of the thin layer of gelatin in the mold. Spread julienned (shredded) slices of **cooked meat or fish**, **vegetables**, **sliced tomatoes**, or whatever your fancy dictates, over the egg slices. Slowly pour on the rest of the gelatin mix.

Cover and put in fridge several hours or, better yet, overnight. This gelée can keep in the fridge for up to three days.

TO UNMOLD: Run a knife blade around the edge, dip bottom of mold briefly in warm water and invert onto a plate.

SUGGESTED COMBINATIONS for ASPICS

- ❖ **Avocado** and **shrimp**
- ❖ **Avocado** and **chicken**
- ❖ **Boiled beef** (pot roast) sliced thin, with **carrots** and **onions** (use the stock the beef was boiled in)
- ❖ **Scallops**, with **avocado** or **shrimp**
- ❖ **Salmon** and **hard-boiled egg** slices
- ❖ Any **fish**, with **peas** and **hard-boiled egg** slices
- ❖ **Ham** with lots and lots of finely chopped **parsley**
- ❖ Add **peas** or **corn** to any of the above combinations.

CHICKEN in ASPIC

Here is an attractive way to use up leftover chicken scraps, or you can substitute ham with lots of parsley for the chicken.

(Serves 6 to 8 people)

From your arsenal		**A mold, 6 to 8 ramekins**, or a **Pyrex pie plate**
Shred	3 cups	**cooked chicken**
Cut in small pieces		
	2-3 thin slices	**ham**, preferably country style

Mix these together in a bowl. Put aside.

Chop finely and put aside		
	1 large bunch	**parsley**
Dissolve together		
	2½ envelopes	**Knox unflavored gelatin**
	½ to ¾ c.	**white wine**
Heat to simmer	2½ c.	**chicken stock**, strong, if possible
	Or 2 to 3	**chicken bouillon cubes** dissolved in 2½ c. water
Stir in	1 tsp.	dried **tarragon**
	Or 1 Tbs.	fresh **tarragon**

Combine the hot stock with softened gelatin mixture to dissolve the gelatin. Let cool a few minutes, but don't let it stiffen.

Pour a little of this broth/wine mixture on the bottom of the mold(s). Sprinkle ½ the chopped parsley over it. Scatter ½ the chicken and ham mixture over it. Sprinkle the rest of the parsley over this. Finish with a layer of chicken/ham mixture.

Pour the broth/wine mixture *slowly* over the whole. Cover and put in fridge for 24 hours.

To unmold, run a knife blade around the edge, dip bottom of mold briefly in warm water and invert on a plate.

––––––––––––––––––

OEUFS EN GELÉE (JELLIED EGGS)

Although this recipe technically doesn't qualify as one for leftovers, I am including it because it is simple to make and demonstrates the technique. It is a big hit every time I serve it. Besides, it's cheap!

(Serves 6)

From your arsenal		**6 ramekins**
		Knox unflavored gelatin
		A saucer

Dissolve together

	2 envelopes	**gelatin**
	¼ c.	**white wine**

Bring to boil 1¾ c. **stock** (chicken or vegetable)

The stock should be clear and strongly seasoned. Add softened gelatin to hot stock. Mix well and let cool to lukewarm.

Pour a little gelatin mix onto the bottom of each ramekin. Decorate with a sprig of parsley, or better, a **tarragon** leaf or two. Strips of **ham** look nice, too.

Have ready 6 **eggs**

Bring a pot of **well-salted water** to a simmer. Break the eggs gently onto a saucer one by one and glide them from the saucer into the simmering water. You can do 2 or 3 eggs at a time. Simmer them for 3 to 4 minutes, gathering the whites around the yolks with a spoon and making sure they don't stick to the bottom.

When they are well set but still runny inside, remove them with a slotted spoon to a paper towel. Let cool.

Place one poached egg in each ramekin. Cover them with the rest of the cooled bouillon. Put in fridge several hours to set. To unmold, run a knife blade around the edge of each custard cup and immerse it briefly in warm water. Invert it onto a lettuce leaf.

Embellish the plate with tomato slices or wedges, small shrimp, or anything else you fancy. But don't overdo it, as the egg should rule in all its glory.

CHAPTER 7: MOUSSES

A mousse is a cross between an aspic/gelée and a timbale (see page 57), as it uses gelatin and cream but leaves out the eggs. It makes a smooth and elegant cold first course or light lunch. The ingredients are put through a blender, mixed with whipped cream, and chilled in buttered molds. It, too, is very easy to make and an unusual way to use up leftover meat, fish, or seafood. I especially like it with fish. You can also add appropriate vegetable leftovers, but please refer to "A Word of Caution" on the following page.

BASIC MOUSSE RECIPE

(Serves 4)

From your arsenal		**4 ramekins** or a **mold**
		Knox unflavored gelatin
		Stock
		White wine
		Whipping cream

Butter the molds and place a sprig of **parsley** on the bottom.

In a cup, dissolve together

| | 1 Tbs. (1 envelope) | **Knox unflavored gelatin** |
| | ¼ c. | **white wine** or **stock** |

In a sauce pan, simmer

	3 Tbs.	**shallots** or **onions**, chopped
	1 Tbs.	**butter**
Add	1 c.	**stock**

Add the soaked gelatin. Bring to simmer. Cool, but not so much that the liquid starts setting. Pour into blender jar.

Add to blender	2 c.	**leftover chicken, ham, or fish**
(Optional)	¼ c.	**leftover vegetables***
	¼ tsp.	**appropriate seasoning****

Blend at top speed till puréed.

In a bowl, beat till just stiff

| | ⅓ c. | **whipping cream** |

Add the blender mixture and whisk until just mixed.

Pour the mixture into the mold(s). Cover and chill in fridge till firm (can be made a day ahead). To unmold, run a knife around the perimeter and immerse briefly in a pan of warm water. Invert onto a plate. You can also invert the cold mold onto a plate and hold a cloth wrung out of hot water around it till it plops onto the plate.

*A WORD of CAUTION! If you are adding vegetables, think about the resulting color of your mousse. It might be better not to purée them but just to layer them in as you pour the purée into the molds.

** Add seasoning according to your leftovers. For example, you may want to add a little lemon juice or tarragon to fish or seafood mixtures.

NOTE: 1 Tbs. (1 envelope) of Knox unflavored gelatin will gel firmly 1 cup of liquid.

SUGGESTIONS

Salmon. Delicious mousse ramekins can be made from last night's supper using baked **salmon**, **zucchini** sautéed with **onions** and **garlic**, and **boiled potatoes**, skin on. Use the cooking water from the potatoes for the stock.

Fish. The above remarks apply to any leftover **fish**. Combine with a **leftover vegetable**, or add some **capers** and a squirt of **lemon juice**.

CHAPTER 8: EGGS

Omelets and frittata are wonderful for a quick lunch or a light supper and are *so* easy to do! All you need are your leftovers and some eggs. Adding grated cheese makes them especially good.

BASIC OMELET

(Serves 2)

In a skillet over medium heat, simmer briefly

1 Tbs.	**shortening**
1 c.	**leftovers**, chopped

Meanwhile in a bowl, beat

3 or 4	**eggs**
1 Tbs.	**water, milk**, or **cream**

Pour egg mixture into skillet. Cook until just set. Fold one side over the other and slide onto platter. Voilà!

You can sprinkle with **grated cheese**. You can also reverse the above procedure by first pouring the egg mixture into the skillet and then adding the leftovers.

Good served with **sliced fresh tomatoes, pickles**, and a slice of **whole wheat toast**.

VARIATION: If you accidentally put in too much liquid, scrub the omelet and just declare it **scrambled eggs**.

––––––––––––

PUFFY OMELET

You can make an omelet lighter by separating the eggs and beating the yolks with the milk or cream. In a separate bowl beat the egg whites with a pinch of salt until they are stiff but still foamy. Fold them into the yolk mixture and cook in skillet until just set. Fold one half over the other and serve.

––––––––––––

BASIC FRITTATA

A frittata is a cross between an omelet and a quiche, as the egg mixture is baked but doesn't have a crust. It is a super-easy way to glorify almost any combination of leftovers. You can use up pieces of **ham**, **sausage**, or **chicken**, or for a vegetarian dish you can incorporate **spinach**, **zucchini**, **broccoli**, **peas**, **green beans**, **mushrooms**, **slices of baked potato** – the list goes on! It is a first cousin to a pudding.

(Serves 4 to 5)

Preheat oven to **350° F.**

In an oven-proof skillet, heat

2 Tbs.	**butter** or **olive oil**

(Optional) Sauté gently

1 to 2	**garlic cloves**, chopped
1 Tbs.	**onion**, chopped

Add and simmer till hot

1 to 2 c.	**leftovers**, chopped (see above for suggestions)

Meanwhile, mix in bowl

4 to 6	**eggs**
2 to 4 Tbs.	**shredded cheese**
	salt & **pepper** (Careful! Check for saltiness of the leftovers.)

Pour egg mixture over leftovers in skillet. Cook on low to medium heat a minute or two till the eggs just begin to set. Place in oven for about 10 minutes.

Or you can cover and continue cooking on the stove over low heat about 10 minutes until eggs are almost set. Sprinkle with grated Parmesan cheese and place under the broiler about 2 minutes.
Remove from broiler and sprinkle with more grated cheese, if desired.

Alternatively, separate the eggs. Beat **whites** until firm and incorporate into egg and cheese mix. This makes for a lighter, almost soufflé-like, quality.

Let stand a few minutes. Cut into wedges.

SUGGESTION: You can make a hearty three-course meal out of one frittata by incorporating cooked **rice, cottage cheese**, a little **milk** or **half & half**. Don't forget to use grated **nutmeg** to enhance the flavor, especially if you are using **spinach**.

MICROWAVE FRITTATA
(Serves 2 to 3)

Melt in glass pie dish

	1 Tbs.	**butter**
Spread with	1 to 1½ c.	**leftovers**, chopped
Stir in	4	**eggs**
		salt & **pepper**

Cover. Cook on **High, 1 to 2 minutes**. Let stand 3 minutes. Cut into wedges.

HARD-BOILED EGGS in CHEESE or CURRY SAUCE
(Serves 3 to 4)

If you need to use up some hard-boiled eggs before they spoil, here is a quick way to rescue them by making a tasty luncheon dish.

Slice crosswise	4 to 6	**hard-boiled eggs**

Spread them on the bottom of a greased ovenproof dish.

Cover them with	1 c.	**Mornay sauce** (shredded cheese added to a béchamel; see page 10)
		Or **curry sauce** (See page 11, but leave out the apples.)

Put under a medium broiler till top is lightly browned and mixture bubbly. Serve the egg-cheese combination with a **tomato salad** and the curry one with a **cucumber salad** (see page 39).

NOTE: These quantities are flexible, depending on how many hard-boiled eggs you have left over.

VARIATION: If you have some **stale bread**, toast it and spread it on the bottom of the baking dish and cover with the egg mixture.

EGGS *EN COCOTTE*

Here is a quick way to use up some sour milk or cream and a few scraps of cooked vegetables or ham.

Preheat oven to **350°** F.
Grease one **ramekin** per egg.

Fill a baking pan with about one inch of water and put in oven to heat.

Place in each one of greased ramekins, in this order

1 Tbs.	**leftover vegetables or ham**, chopped
1	**egg**
1 to 2 Tbs.	**sour milk** or **cream**, to cover
A few dots	**butter**
1 Tbs.	**grated cheese**
	a garnish, such as a piece of **ham** or an **asparagus tip**

Place ramekins in the baking pan and bake for about **15 minutes**. The egg should be cooked but its interior still runny.

EGG NESTS

The number of eggs will depend on the amount of **leftover spinach** you are using.

In a skillet, simmer together briefly

	1 Tbs.	**shortening or butter**
	1 Tbs.	**onions**, chopped
Add	1 to 2 c.	**cooked spinach**

Make dents in the spinach mixture and drop an egg into each nest. Top the eggs with **grated cheese**, **bacon bits**, or **ham pieces**. Cover and cook about 3 minutes. Or you can put the skillet under a medium broiler for about 3 minutes, until the eggs are cooked but the yolks still runny.

CHAPTER 9: QUICHES/PIZZAS

A quiche is basically unsweetened custard baked in a pie crust. You can quickly make a delicious first course or light lunch meal by combining your meat and/or vegetable leftovers with an egg and cream mixture, pouring it into a partially baked pie crust, and baking it for about 35 minutes. I like to keep store-bought frozen deep-dish pie crusts on hand, but you can always make your own. (See below.)

From your arsenal   **A pie crust**
                                    Eggs
                                    Cream or **half and half**
                                    Grated cheese (optional)

BASIC PIE CRUST for QUICHE
           (Makes two crusts for 9-inch pie plate)
Best if you use   **a food processor**. Use cutting blade.

Mix lightly in processor

	2 c.	**flour**, sifted
	½ tsp.	**baking powder**
	¼ tsp.	**salt**

Cut into chunks and add

	4 oz. (1 stick)	**butter**
	3 Tbs.	**Crisco***

Pulse very briefly. Stop when mixture resembles coarse gravel. If you don't have a processor, cut in the shortening with a pastry cutter or two knives.

Add gradually   3 to 4 Tbs.   **ice water**
Pulse a few times. If still too dry, add more drops of ice water. Stop before dough becomes sticky.

* Crisco is the magic ingredient in a tender and succulent crust. You can tweak the butter/Crisco ratio, but remember that butter provides the luscious flavor!

Turn out on a cold, floured surface. Knead quickly with heel of hand (the palm is too warm) until dough holds together in a ball. It is important to keep the dough as cold as possible. Wrap and put in fridge for about 1 hour. It's even better if frozen, in which case you have to thaw it at room temperature for about 1 hour before continuing.

Preheat oven to **400° F.**

Cut the dough ball in half and roll out one of the halves on a lightly-floured, cold surface. When it's the right size, place in pie pan. Prick bottom with fork. If you have time, chill in fridge for another ½ hour.

The other half can be frozen for future use.

Remove from fridge and grease a sheet of aluminum foil. Press the greased side against the crust and cover with a half-inch of dried beans or pie crust weights. Or you can grease the bottom of a heavy pie plate of the same size and place it on the crust.

Bake for **15 minutes**. Cool before adding filling.

NOTE: The basic ratio of flour to shortening is 3:1. For a crumblier crust, you can add 1 Tbs. shortening.

BASIC QUICHE FILLING

(Makes an 9-inch deep dish pie for 4 to 6 people)

Preheat oven to **375° F.**

Have ready		**a cooled, partially baked pie crust**
		(see above recipe or use store-bought)
	1 to 1½ c.	**leftovers,** chopped

If the leftovers are very moist, sprinkle them with flour.

Beat together	3	**eggs**
	1 c.	**cream** or **half & half**
	1 Tbs.	**white wine**
	½	**onion,** minced and lightly sautéed (to jazz up your leftovers if too bland)
(Optional, depending on leftovers)		
	1 Tbs.	**tomato paste**

Spread your cut-up leftovers on the bottom of the pie shell. If leftovers are very moist, sprinkle with 1 Tbs. **flour.** Pour on the egg mixture. Dot with butter or margarine and sprinkle with **grated cheese**, if desired.

Bake for about **35 minutes** or until the quiche is golden brown and puffy. A toothpick inserted into it should come out clean. Best served **lukewarm**.

NOTE: The basic ratio of eggs to liquid is 3 to 1 cup. You may need to adjust this according to the moisture of your leftovers (by adding another egg). You can partially bake the pie crust and refrigerate the filling ahead of time. About an hour before serving, combine and bake.

EASY QUICHE, with TORTILLA

Here is a quick recipe using a leftover tortilla, or you can use a partially baked pastry crust.

Preheat oven to **350°** F.

Warm		**a large tortilla**
Mix in bowl		**4 eggs**
	1 c. (8 oz.)	**sour cream**
	Add	**any leftover odds & ends**

Put the warm tortilla in a pie pan and spread the mixture on it. Bake for about **30 minutes**.

PIZZAS

A quick pizza can be assembled with assorted meat leftovers and staples that you have on hand. If you don't have a frozen pizza crust, a regular pie crust can do. You can also use a package of refrigerator crescent rolls, pressed to fit a pie pan.

Preheat oven to **400°** F.

Spread a partially baked **pizza or pie crust** with **tomato or pasta sauce**.
Spread with cut up **meat leftovers**. If not enough, fry some **bacon** or **ground beef**.
Add cooked **mushrooms, spinach, green** or **red peppers**, or any appropriate **veggie leftovers**.
Cover with **grated cheese**. (This is a good way to use up cheese scraps.)
Put in oven for about **15 minutes**.

CHAPTER 10: SOUFFLÉS

Now, don't groan! A soufflé is actually quite simple and is a glamorous way to use up your leftovers. The only hitch is that you have to serve it immediately after it comes out of the oven. But you can prepare most of it ahead of time and then combine it with the beaten egg whites at the last minute. The principle is basically this: a thick **béchamel** is combined with **egg yolks** and your **leftovers**, and then combined with beaten **egg whites**. What could be simpler?

BASIC SOUFFLÉ RECIPE
(Serves 4 to 5)

Preheat oven to **400°** F.

Grease the bottom and sides of a	**6-cup soufflé dish** or **any straight-sided oven-proof dish**
Sprinkle with	**bread crumbs** or **grated cheese**

In a large saucepan, make

	1 c.	**thick white sauce** (3:3:1. See page 8.)
Add and mix	¾ c. to 1 c.	**leftovers**, chopped
Separate	4	**eggs** (preferably at room temperature)

Beat one **egg yolk** at a time into the white sauce in the sauce pan over low heat and drop the whites into a large, deep bowl. Be sure to keep the whites squeaky clean. (They will not rise if there is even a trace of yolk.)
Allow this mixture to cool for a few minutes.

Beat at low speed till foaming		**the 4 egg whites**, plus one or two more, if available
(Optional) Add	¼ tsp.	**cream of tartar** (makes the beaten whites firmer)
Add	pinch	**salt**

Continue beating the egg whites at high speed, tipping and rotating the bowl to get an even blend of whites and air, until they are so stiff that they form peaks that flop over a tiny bit.

Gently fold a little of the whites into the cooled white sauce mixture in the pan. Return this mixture to the whites and fold together very gently. The ingredients should be well mixed but still light and fluffy.

Pour into the prepared oven-proof dish.

Put in oven and lower the temperature to **375°** F. Do not open oven door for at least **25 minutes**! The soufflé should be nice and brown and puffy after 35 minutes. Turn off oven. The soufflé will keep for about 5 minutes as you hurry your guests or family to the table.

To serve, cut into the center of the soufflé vertically.

NOTE: Depending on your leftovers, you can use stock, bouillon, water from cooked vegetables, milk, cream, even **slightly sour milk**, or a combination of these for the béchamel liquid. You can enhance the flavor of your leftovers by adding **sautéed chopped onions** mixed with a dash of flour or some **tomato paste** and **white wine**. **Grated cheese** is another tasty addition. Have fun playing with the combinations, but be careful not to exceed 1 cup of leftover ingredients.

SUGGESTIONS for SOUFFLÉS

❖ Ground **ham**. Add a dash of mustard to the white sauce.
❖ **Spinach**. Make sure it's not too moist. Add ¼ cup grated mild **Swiss cheese** and some grated **nutmeg**.
❖ **Corn**, well drained
❖ Chopped **broccoli**. Use milk for the white sauce. Sprinkle with grated cheese.
❖ **Asparagus spears** cut into 1-inch pieces, mixed with ¼ cup grated mild **Swiss cheese**
❖ **Fish**, especially salmon, shrimp. If available, use fish or shrimp stock for the béchamel. Tarragon is good flavoring.
❖ **Chicken, garlic**, and grated **cheese**. Mince the chicken fine.
❖ Any mixture of chopped **cooked vegetables** combined with a little grated **raw carrot and celery**

IMPROVISED SOUFFLÉ, with DUMPLINGS

If you are stuck with leftover **mashed potatoes** or you made too many **dumplings**, you can adjust them to be the base for a soufflé. See the recipe on page 111 for Mock Potato Soufflé to use mashed potatoes. For dumplings follow this procedure.

Preheat oven to **375° F.**

Grease		**a soufflé dish** or a **straight-sided casserole**
(Optional) Sprinkle with		**bread crumbs** or **grated cheese**

In a large saucepan beat together

	about 2 c.	**leftover dumplings**, crumbled
	3	**egg yolks**
	⅓ to ½ c.	**half & half**, enough to make a thick and smooth creamy sauce. Add more if necessary.
Add	½ to ¾ c.	**leftovers**, chopped or **grated cheese**

Adjust the seasoning. Try a grating of **nutmeg**. Heat this mixture over low heat, stirring well and taking care not to let it come to the boil. Let it cool a bit.

Beat until very firm

	3	**egg whites** (more, if available)
	pinch	**salt**

Fold the beaten egg whites into the mixture in the saucepan and pour into the prepared baking dish. Bake for **30 to 35 minutes**. Remember not to open the oven door for at least 25 minutes!

———————————

CHAPTER 11: TIMBALES

The modern concept of a timbale is a custard containing chopped-up cooked vegetables, meat, or seafood. Thus it lends itself successfully to using up tasty leftovers and is incredibly delicious. The mixture is poured into a ring mold, wide bowl, or individual ramekins and set into a pan of simmering water in the oven. Individual molds take about 35 minutes, a ring or a bowl about 45 minutes, in a 325°F oven. Individual timbales make an elegant first course. The first two recipes are custard-like. The third is a variation with a richer and denser texture.

Here is an example of what can be done with some leftover vegetables, in this case a few asparagus spears and some braised carrots. Spinach also makes a delicious timbale.

TIMBALE of CARROTS and ASPARAGUS
(Makes 5 to 6 ramekins)

Preheat oven to **325° F.**

Grease   **5 to 6 ramekins** or a **mold**

Place a **rack** or folded towel on the bottom of a large **ovenproof pan**. Fill with 1 to 2 inches of **water** and place in middle of oven to heat.

Warm on **High** in microwave for about **30 seconds** and put aside

	1½ c.	**half & half** (or a **cream** and **stock** mix)
Mix in bowl	4	**eggs**
	¾ tsp.	**salt**
	½ tsp.	**paprika**
	1 Tbs.	**onion**, minced
	1 Tbs.	**parsley**, chopped
Add	1 to 1½ c.	**cooked carrots** and **asparagus**, chopped
Add		**the warm cream**

Pour mixture into buttered mold(s) and place on rack or folded towel in the pan of simmering water. Bake till custard is set, about **30 to 50 minutes**, depending on the size of the mold(s).

When set, remove mold(s) from water and let partially cool on a rack. Run a knife around the edge and turn onto a plate. Best if served lukewarm. The timbale(s) can be stored in the fridge and reheated in the microwave oven.

The proportion of 4 eggs to 1½ cup cream can be used to incorporate other leftovers, such as chopped **meats**, **fish**, and **seafood**. Use your imagination to season the custard mix with appropriate seasonings, e.g. **cilantro**, **nutmeg**, **lemon juice**.

NOTE: If appropriate, you can serve with a **tomato sauce** or store-bought pasta sauce.

CRABMEAT TIMBALES

Perhaps you have some fresh crabmeat left over from another meal. If you want to use it in a light recipe that will not overwhelm its delicate flavor, you can use the basic procedure above with slight variations in quantities.

(Serves 4)

Preheat oven to **350°** F.

Grease   4 **ramekins** or a medium-sized **mold**

Place a **rack** or folded towel on the bottom of a large **ovenproof pan**. Fill with 1 to 2 inches of **water** and place in middle of oven to heat.

Warm in microwave oven

1 c.	**half & half** (or a **cream** and **stock** mix)

Beat together in a bowl

3	**eggs**
½ tsp.	**salt**
¼ tsp.	**pepper**
1 Tbs.	**onion**, minced
1 Tbs.	**celery**, minced
1 Tbs.	**parsley**, chopped
1 tsp.	**dried tarragon**

Stir in gently   8 oz.   **crab meat**

Add the warm cream/stock and mix gently.

Pour into the ramekins. Place on the rack or folded towel in the pan of simmering water and put in oven. Bake till custard is set, about **30 to 50 minutes**, depending on the size of the mold(s).

When set, remove mold(s) from water and let partially cool on a rack. Run a knife around the edge and turn onto a plate. Best if served lukewarm. They can be stored in the fridge and reheated in the microwave oven.

NOTE: In general, the ratio is 1 cup **leftovers** per 1 cup **half & half** per 3 **eggs**.

SUGGESTIONS

- ❖ **Fish** and **spinach** (e.g. chopped-up swordfish and creamed spinach)
- ❖ **Ham** and **broccoli**
- ❖ **Chicken** and assorted **vegetables**
- ❖ **Seafood**, with or without a vegetable
- ❖ **Chicken, garlic**, and **cheese**
- ❖ **Fish**, flavored with a little lemon and lots of **cilantro**
- ❖ **Fish** and **mushrooms**
- ❖ See page 171 for **Fruit Timbales**.

TIMBALE VARIATION

With this method you will use a béchamel as a base.

(Serves 4)

Preheat oven to **350°** F.

Grease   **4 ramekins** or a **small mold**

Place a **rack** or folded towel on the bottom of a large **ovenproof pan**. Fill with about 1 inch of **water** and place in middle of oven to heat.

Make   ½ c.   **medium béchamel**, using vegetable, meat, chicken, or fish **stock**, if available (1:1:½, see page 8)

Put in blender and process at top speed

                    1 c.   **leftovers**, see suggestions above

                    1   **egg**

| | 1 | **egg yolk** (the white can go into your next scrambled eggs) |

Add the béchamel along with

| | 3 Tbs. | **heavy cream** |
| (Optional) | 1 Tbs. | **wine** or **cognac**, according to your leftovers |

Blend briefly at top speed.

Pour mixture into prepared ramekins or mold and place in a pan containing about one inch of hot water. Bake for **20 to 25 minutes** for the ramekins and **35 to 40 minutes** for the mold.

When set, remove mold(s) from water and let partially cool on a rack. Run a knife around the edge and turn onto a plate. Best if served lukewarm. They can be stored in the fridge and reheated in the microwave oven.

Serve with an appropriate sauce, e.g. **béarnaise**, **mushroom**, **tomato** (see pages 11, 14, 16).

SALMON TIMBALES

(Serves 4)

Following the above procedure for crabmeat timbales,

Make	¾ c.	**medium béchamel** (1½:1½:¾)
Add and mix	2	**eggs**
	1 c.	**cooked salmon**, flaked
	2 Tbs.	**heavy cream**

Process briefly in blender and pour into 4 greased ramekins or a small mold. Place in a pan containing about one inch of hot water.

Bake for **20 to 25 minutes** for the ramekins and **35 to 40 minutes** for the mold.

Reverse onto serving plates and serve with a **mushroom or tomato sauce** (see pages 11, 14).

CHAPTER 12: CRÊPES & PANCAKES

Stuffed crêpes are an easy and elegant way to present many different kinds of leftovers. People go crazy over them. They are quite filling. You make a semi-thick or thick béchamel (depending on the moisture of your leftovers), mix it with your chopped-up leftovers, season it appropriately, and spread the mix on crêpes. Roll them up and place in a buttered oven-proof dish. Cover them amply with a light béchamel, sprinkle with grated cheese, if appropriate, and put them in the oven for about half an hour.

STUFFED CRÊPES

From your arsenal

Crêpes, which you can make any time and refrigerate or freeze
Thick and thin béchamels
A blender
A crêpe or regular small skillet
A pastry brush (not with nylon bristles, as they will melt)
Filling according to your leftovers

BASIC CRÊPE RECIPE

(Makes ten to twelve 7-inch crêpes)

Melt   2 Tbs. (¼ stick) **butter**

Put in blender in this order

½ c.	**water** and ½ c. **milk**
Or 1 c.	**skimmed milk**
2	**eggs**
¼ tsp.	**salt**
¾ c.	**flour**
	the melted butter

Blend **1 minute** on **High**. Refrigerate for at least 1 hour.

NOTE: For sweetened crêpes, add 1 Tbs. **sugar.**

COOKING THE CRÊPES

Heat a 6- to 8-inch **frying** or **crêpe** or **omelet pan** over medium heat.
Put a little **cooking oil** (not olive) in a dish, ready to grease the pan with.
Have ready a **pastry brush** (natural bristles).
Brush a little oil on the bottom of the pan when it's quite hot.
Pour in just enough batter to coat the bottom, tipping the pan to spread the batter evenly. Pour off any excess.

Cook for **15 to 20 seconds**, until the crêpe almost stops steaming. Flip it over, with a spatula if necessary, and cook another **10 to 15** seconds.
Turn out on a plate and brush the pan lightly again with the oil.

Repeat above procedure till all the batter is used up.
Regulate the heat as you go along to prevent burning.

NOTE: The first 2 or 3 crêpes might not be the best because you will be fine tuning the heat of the pan and the thickness of the film of batter. But they make excellent nibbling!

FILLING for CRÊPES

Make a **semi-thick béchamel** (2½:2½:1; see page 8) and gently mix in about 1 cup of your **leftovers**. If your leftovers are very moist, make a thick béchamel (3:3:1).

Spread on as many crêpes as you need. One cup of béchamel mixed with one cup of leftovers will fill eight to ten crêpes.

Roll them up and place seam side down in a buttered oven-proof dish. Cover with a sauce, as follows.

SAUCE for STUFFED CRÊPES

Make 1 to 2 cups **light béchamel** (1½:1½:1; see page 8) using milk or stock appropriate for your leftovers. Make plenty to cover the crêpes generously. Pour over crêpes. Sprinkle very lightly with grated cheese (optional).

Bake the stuffed crêpes in **350°** F oven for about **30 minutes**, or put them under a medium broiler until they are lightly browned (about 15 minutes).

NOTE: You can use any kind of light sauce over the crêpes. If you stuff them with leftover **meat**, you could cover them with a creamy **tomato sauce** by adding a little tomato paste, tomato or pasta sauce to the light white sauce. Also, upgrade the sauce by adding sautéed **mushrooms** (see pages 12 and 99 for *Duxelles* and Mushroom Preparation).

SUGGESTIONS for STUFFED CRÊPES

❖ **Seafood** and **fish** rolled in crêpes are delicious. Make a semi-thick white sauce (2½:2½:1; see page 8), if possible using saved fish or shrimp stock or a fish bouillon cube. Season with **tarragon, cilantro** and/or **lemon juice**. Or you can use **white wine** or **sherry**.

❖ A **ham** mix or a **chicken** filling is good, too. Cut the meat into very small cubes. Use a lot of chopped **parsley**.

❖ Add cut-up **corn** to the above combinations; enhance with **cumin**.

❖ Or add **peas, asparagus, green beans**, or **carrots**.

❖ Mix pieces of leftover **roast duck** with slivers of **scallions** and **soy sauce**. Make your coating white sauce very light (1:1:1), using chicken stock (not milk).

─────────────

SOUR MILK CRÊPES

If you have milk that has soured, use the above basic crêpe recipe and add ½ tsp. **baking soda** to the flour. You may also substitute one or two **egg whites** for one of the eggs.

─────────────

CRÊPES STUFFED with FISH

Here is a sample of what can be done with a leftover fish filet and a couple of leftover sea scallops. My hope is that this will inspire you to try many different combinations and clean out your refrigerator containers at the same time.

(Serves 4 to 6)

Start by mixing a batch of crêpes (see above, page 61). While the batter is maturing in the fridge, make the following filling and sauce.

For the FILLING

Make	1c.	**béchamel** (2:2:1, see page 8), using vegetable stock

Add and mix gently

	1 c.	**cooked fish**, flaked
	1	**hard-boiled egg**
	1 tsp.	**dried tarragon**
(Optional)	1 to 2 Tbs.	**mushrooms**, chopped

Put aside.

For the SAUCE

Make a **béchamel** using

	1½ Tbs.	**butter**
	1½ Tbs.	**flour**
	½ c.	**vegetable stock**
	½ c.	**half & half**
	¼ c.	**canned tomato sauce**

Put aside.

To ASSEMBLE

Cook the crêpes according to the directions on page 62. You will need 8 to 12 crêpes.

One by one, cover each crêpe half way with the filling. Roll it up and place seam side down in a greased oven-proof serving dish.

Pour the sauce over all the crêpes and sprinkle lightly with breadcrumbs, if desired.

Bake the stuffed crêpes in **350°** F oven for about **30 minutes**, or put them under a medium broiler until they are lightly browned (about **15 minutes**).

———————

CRÊPES or WAFFLES with SOUR MILK or CREAM

Another way to use up sour milk is to adapt the basic crêpe recipe above
(page 61) by adding

1 tsp.	**sugar**
¾ tsp.	**baking powder**
½ tsp.	**baking soda**

to the dry ingredients. Use the same amount of liquid. This will make puffy
crêpes.

If you are making waffles, separate the eggs and fold in the beaten whites
at the end.

See **CHAPTER 30: FRUIT, page 168 for recipe using sweet crêpes.**

CORN PANCAKES or FRITTERS

Corn fritters are a classic, and although the usual recipes call for fresh corn,
yesterday's corn dish can be metamorphosed quite easily into fritters that melt
in your mouth. They can be cooked like pancakes or deep fried when made
with heavier dough (see Chapter 14, page 73).

There are many approaches, but here are a couple of suggestions.

SIMPLE CORN PANCAKES or FRITTERS
            (Makes about eight 3-inch pancakes)
Mix together in bowl

1½ c.	**cut cooked corn** (from about 2 medium-sized cobs)
3	**eggs**
1½ tsp.	**baking powder**
6 Tbs.	**flour**
½ tsp.	**salt**

Drop mixture by spoonfuls on lightly-greased griddle or skillet. Serve like
pancakes with plenty of butter and syrup.

NOTE: You can process the corn along with 1 Tbs. **milk** or **stock** in a
blender for a smoother batter.

CORN FRITTERS, PAN FRIED

(Makes about fourteen 3-inch fritters)

Separate into 2 bowls

	2	**eggs**

Beat the yolks. Add

	2½ c.	**cut cooked corn** (from about 4 cobs)
Add and stir in	1 Tbs.	**sugar**
	pinches	**salt** and **pepper**
	¼ tsp.	**ground cumin**
	2 Tbs.	**flour**

Beat until very firm the 2 egg whites.
Incorporate the beaten egg whites into the corn mixture. (Not the other way around.)

Heat in skillet	2 Tbs.	**butter** or **oil**

Drop batter by tablespoonfuls into hot fat and fry 1 to 2 minutes on each side over medium heat. Serve with a **hot chili-based sauce** or **maple syrup**.

CORN FRITTERS, SOUTHERN STYLE

Even simpler is this "Southern style" method.

(Makes about fifteen 3-inch fritters)

Mix	about 2½ c.	**cut cooked corn** (from 4 ears)
	4	**eggs**, beaten
	½ c.	**flour**
	½ tsp.	**salt**

Fry in hot butter or oil like pancakes.

OTHER PANCAKES

VEGETABLE CAKES

Use the recipes for Simple Corn Pancakes (see page 65) or Corn Fritters (see above) and substitute cut-up cooked vegetables. If they are very moist, increase the flour slightly.

FISH CAKES with AÏOLI or CAPER SAUCE

A stand-by with my family is Crab Cakes, but since we are talking about leftovers, I have adapted my favorite crab cake recipe to accommodate that odd piece of fish filet that nobody wanted to finish last night. We enjoy crab or fish cakes with an aïoli or a caper sauce.

For the FISH CAKES

(Makes 4 to 5 three-inch patties)

Mix together in a bowl

2 Tbs.	**celery**, chopped
2 Tbs.	**onion**, chopped
3 Tbs.	**bread crumbs**
1	**egg**
1 Tbs.	**lemon juice**
2 Tbs.	**mayonnaise** (homemade preferred)
pinch	**salt** and **pepper**

Add and mix in well

1¾ to 2 c.	**cooked fish**, flaked

In a skillet, over low to medium flame, heat about 1 Tbs. **vegetable oil** with 1 tsp. **sesame seed oil**.

(Optional) Spread on a plate   **bread crumbs**

With your hands make patties about 1 inch thick. They will be very moist. If you are not watching your calories, coat them lightly with the bread crumbs.

Sauté the cakes about 3 minutes on each side, taking care not to burn the bread crumbs if you are using them. Transfer patties to a dish to keep warm.

For an AÏOLI SAUCE

In a small bowl whisk together

½ c.	**mayonnaise**
½ tsp.	**Tabasco or hot sauce**
2 cloves	**garlic**, crushed
2 tsp.	**lemon juice**

Adjust the proportions and the seasoning according to your taste. Add a little **salt and/or pepper** if necessary.

For a CAPER SAUCE

In the same pan you have sautéed the fish cakes in, over medium heat

Melt	2 Tbs.	**butter**
Stir in	1½ Tbs.	**flour**
Add and mix vigorously		
	1¼ to 1½ c.	**vegetable stock**
Add	1 Tbs.	**Dijon mustard**
	1 Tbs.	**capers**
	1 Tbs.	**sour or dill pickles**, chopped

Simmer for a few minutes. If too stiff, add a little stock or hot water. The sauce should be light but not runny. Spoon over the fish cakes.

———————

CHAPTER 13: TORTILLAS & WRAPS

Tortillas can be adapted to all sorts of Mexican dishes: burritos, tacos, quesadillas, and enchiladas, to name only a few. They are an obvious way to use up chopped leftover **meat, chicken, fish**, or **seafood**. Jazz up the filling with an assortment of **shredded cheese, salsa, mashed beans, mashed garbanzos, garlic, chopped onion, chopped tomatoes, green peppers, chili peppers, shredded lettuce, chopped cooked spinach, guacamole** and **sour cream**. If you have some **taco seasoning mix**, all the better.

BASIC QUESADILLA PROCEDURE
(Serves 2)

You will need	4 small (7-inch)	**flour tortillas**
	1 c.	**shredded cheese**

Any mild or Monterey Jack cheese will do. You can use a mixture of shredded pieces of leftover cheese.

Cut into strips	½ c.	**cooked chicken or turkey**
Mix in a bowl	1 Tbs.	**cilantro**, chopped
	1 Tbs.	**onion**, chopped
	¼ tsp.	**powdered cumin**
	½ Tbs.	**jalapeño pepper**, minced
(Optional)	½ c.	**cooked mushrooms**, chopped
(Optional)	¼ c.	**green pepper**, chopped
(Optional)	¼ c.	**cooked corn**
Add		**the chicken and turkey strips**
Heat in skillet over medium heat		
	1 Tbs.	**vegetable oil**

Place a tortilla in skillet. Spread with half the chicken mixture and half the shredded cheese. Cover with another tortilla and cook for a minute. Turn the whole thing and cook another minute or until the cheese melts.

Put aside and keep warm while making the other quesadilla. When done, cut into wedges and serve with guacamole (see below), sour cream, and salsa.

NOTE: If you are using 2 large flour tortillas, spread the chicken and cheese on half the tortilla, cook a minute, fold over the other half, flip, and cook another minute. Cut into wedges.

BASIC GUACAMOLE

(Makes about 1½ cups)

In a bowl, fork mash

	2 ripe	**Haas avocados**
	Or 1	large **avocado**
Add and mix	1 Tbs.	**lemon** or **lime juice**
Add	1 clove	**garlic**, mashed
	¼	**onion**, chopped
	Or 2	chopped **scallions**
	2 Tbs.	**cilantro**, chopped
	pinch	**salt**
(Optional)	1 small	**tomato**, chopped
(Optional)	¼ tsp.	**Tabasco**

Mix well with a fork. Serve at room temperature, but store in fridge.

SUGGESTION: If you leave avocados in chunks and add a pinch of cumin, you can use them with cooked **shrimp** or **crabmeat** for delicious quesadillas. Spread the tortilla with a layer of avocado mix, some seafood, some canned green chili peppers (optional), and shredded cheese. Proceed as in the basic quesadilla recipe above.

ENCHILADAS

Enchiladas are another version of the stuffed tortilla scenario. You can use corn or flour tortillas. Again, use your imagination, limited only by your arsenal and supply of leftovers. Use the ingredients suggested in the chapter introduction and in previous recipes.

Preheat oven to **350°** F.

Warm tortillas according to instructions on package.

Spread an ovenproof dish with a thin layer of tomato-based **salsa**.

Place meat or seafood mix, cheese, and seasonings (see chapter introduction above) on one side of small tortilla. Roll. Place seam side down in dish. Top with generous amount of **salsa** and sprinkle with shredded cheese.

Bake for about **20 minutes**. Let stand 5 minutes. Serve with **sour cream**.

CHILAQUILES

These are an interesting use of **corn tortillas**. In this recipe you will use pieces of cooked **chicken** or **turkey** and **tomatillos**, which are like small green tomatoes in a brown casing.

(Serves 5 to 6)

You will need   **a blender** or **food processor**

Preheat oven to **350°** F.

Have ready   2 c.   **shredded cheese**

Remove the casings and soak in water 5 minutes

                           1 lb.   **tomatillos**

Dry them, cut in half, and remove cores. Put in blender.

Add   ¼   **onion**, chopped

                           ¼ c.   **fresh cilantro**

                           1   **jalapeño chile pepper**, seeded

                           3 to 4 cloves   **garlic**

Blend at medium speed till smooth. Add a pinch of salt, if necessary.

Pour into skillet or large saucepan and simmer this sauce over low heat for about **10 minutes**.

Meanwhile, cut or tear into strips

                           10   **small corn tortillas**

Heat in skillet   ¼ c.   **canola oil**

Cook tortilla strips for 1 to 2 minutes over medium heat. Don't overcrowd. When crisp and golden brown, put on paper towel to drain off fat.

When tomatillo sauce is well cooked, stir in

                           about 2 c.   **cooked chicken or turkey pieces**

Grease a 9- x 12-inch baking dish. Spread bottom with a layer of half the tortilla strips. Add a layer of half the tomatillo and chicken mixture. Add half the shredded cheese.

Repeat, topping with a layer of shredded cheese. Bake for about **30 minutes**. Let stand for 5 minutes.

BURRITOS

Burritos, made with warmed flour tortillas, are an even simpler way to use up leftover **chicken, seafood,** or **ground meat** (you can also use **meat loaf**). Follow instructions on package for warming the tortillas.

Meanwhile, in a bowl, add a spoonful of **salsa** and some **shredded lettuce** to any or all of the ingredients listed in the chapter introduction. If you have some **taco seasoning mix**, by all means add it.

Spoon mixture onto middle of a small warmed taco and fold over towards the center: first the top, then the bottom, then the two sides, overlapping them. Serve.

WRAPS

Wraps are another use for **flour tortillas**. For a colorful touch, add leftover **spinach** to the ingredients listed in the chapter introduction. **Barbecue sauce** is a moisturizing addition. Place the ingredients in the middle of a small flour tortilla. Wrap it as if you were making a burrito (see above) and place in a square of aluminum foil, seam side down.

Wrap the aluminum foil around it and place in oven-proof dish. Place in a **350°** F oven for about **10 minutes**.

CHAPTER 14: FRITTERS & CROQUETTES

Fritters and croquettes are first cousins. Both are deep fried. If you prepare them correctly, the fat content should not be very high. They are a delicious way to recycle cooked vegetables and meats.

FRITTERS are a mix of chopped leftovers, using egg and flour as binders, whereas **CROQUETTES** are made with a binding béchamel base or cream puff paste dough. You will need a deep fat fryer filled with enough clean cooking oil to allow the croquettes or fritters to float. I will start with the simplest recipe.

From your arsenal

Deep fat fryer, or any deep sauce pan
Cooking oil (vegetable or canola, not olive)
Thermometer
Slotted spoon

FRITTERS

BASIC VEGETABLE FRITTERS
(Makes twelve to fifteen 2-inch fritters)

Beat in medium bowl

	1	**egg**
Beat in	1 c.	**cooked vegetables**, minced
	2 Tbs.	**butter**, melted
	2 Tbs.	**flour**
	1 to 5 Tbs.	**milk** or **stock**, depending on moisture of your leftovers
	¼ tsp.	**Worcester sauce** or **lemon juice**
	1 Tbs.	**parsley**, chopped, and/or **fresh herbs**

You should have a stiff mixture. If too moist, increase the flour a little. Spread mixture on a greased dish and cool in fridge for about an hour. When cold, shape into small balls or oblongs, between 1 to 2 inches.

Have ready	1 plate	**flour**
	1 shallow dish	**1 egg** beaten with 1 Tbs. **water**
	1 plate	**bread crumbs**

Start slowly preheating the deep fat oil to **365°** F

Roll the balls in flour; shake off excess flour; dip them into the egg mixture, making sure they're completely coated; roll them in the bread crumbs. You can put them on a rack to dry for about 15 minutes, if you have time.

When oil temperature reaches **365°** F, deep fry a few at a time, leaving plenty of space for the balls to expand. Keep a close watch on them, as they only take a couple of minutes to reach a golden brown color.

Remove with slotted spoon and put on paper towel to absorb excess fat. Keep warm till serving.

Nice with a **tomato sauce**, an **Asian sauce**, or even **ketchup**.

NOTE: When you have finished frying, strain the fat through a fine sieve or paper towel into a can, which will keep in the fridge for weeks. You can reuse this fat three or four times, straining it each time.

CORN FRITTERS, DEEP FRIED
(Serves 4)

Slowly heat in a deep pan to **360°** F.

	deep fat cooking oil (not olive)

Combine in a bowl and beat

1	**egg yolk**
⅓ c.	**flour**
½ tsp.	**salt**
½ tsp.	**baking powder**
¼ tsp.	**paprika** or **cumin**
½ c.	**corn**, cream style*

Beat until stiff	1	**egg white**

Fold in the egg yolk mixture.

Drop by spoonful into the hot cooking oil and cook at **360°** F for about **3 minutes**.

* You can make your own cream style corn with ½ cup **béchamel** (see page 8) and kernels from one cooked **corn cob**.

CROQUETTES

Croquettes use finely chopped cooked food and are deep fried like fritters, but their binding agent is usually a thick béchamel (binding béchamel) or a *pâte à choux*. One or two egg yolks can be added to the thick béchamel for enrichment and extra binding. As with fritters, you can use leftover meat, chicken, seafood, or vegetables. Start by making a binding béchamel (3:5½:1; see page 9). As with fritters, you will need to thoroughly cool the mixture before shaping it; then if you have time, you should let the prepared croquettes dry on a rack before immersing them in the deep frying fat.

For expediency's sake, I am repeating the recipe for binding béchamel from page 9.

BINDING BÉCHAMEL

Follow the procedure on page 8 for making a béchamel, but use a ratio of **3: 5½:1** (3 Tbs. shortening: 5½ Tbs. flour: 1 cup liquid) to obtain a binding béchamel. If possible, use a liquid appropriate for your leftovers, e.g. chicken stock for chicken or vegetables. Cook gently till there is no more flour taste. Keep warm till used.

BASIC CROQUETTE RECIPE
(Makes about twelve 2-inch croquettes)

In a large sauce pan, make

1 c.	**binding béchamel**

Over very low heat, beat in

	1 or 2	**egg yolks**
Stir in	2 c.	**cooked meat**, **fish**, **chicken**, or **veggies**, minced

Add any appropriate seasoning: **herbs or spices**; **chopped parsley**, **onions**, **or garlic**; **Worchester sauce**; **lemon juice**. Check for saltiness before adding salt.

Beat until the mixture binds together. Spread on a greased platter and put in fridge until thoroughly chilled.

Meanwhile prepare

1 plate	**flour**
1 shallow dish	1 **egg** beaten with 1 Tbs. of **water** and 1 Tbs. canola **oil**
1 plate	**bread crumbs**

Start slowly preheating the deep frying oil to **365°** F.

Cut the chilled dough into oblongs about 2 inches long, the size of a wine bottle cork. Roll them in the flour; shake off excess flour; dip them into the egg mixture, making sure they're completely coated. Finally, roll them in the bread crumbs, making sure the crumbs adhere. If you like, you can repeat the egg and bread crumb maneuver to secure the coating. Work lightly with your fingers, using a spoon to help if necessary. Place the croquettes on a rack to dry for about 15 minutes, if you have time.

When oil temperature reaches **365°** F, deep fry a few at a time, leaving plenty of space for the balls to expand. Keep a close watch on them, as they only take a couple of minutes to reach a golden brown color. Remove with slotted spoon and put on paper towel to absorb excess fat. Keep warm till serving. If you have to reheat them, use a 450° F oven.

NOTE: You can use 1 cup leftover **mashed potatoes** instead of the binding béchamel. Use a **whole egg**.

SUGGESTIONS

- ❖ **Rice** and **cheese**
- ❖ Add minced **mushrooms** (or *Duxelles*, page 12) to your leftover mix.

CROQUETTES MADE with *PÂTE À CHOUX*

Another way to make croquettes is to use cream puff paste, a.k.a. *pâte à choux*, instead of a binding béchamel, as a base. Learning to make a *pâte à choux* is almost as important as mastering the art of making a béchamel and almost as easy. It can be used as a base for all sorts of dishes besides croquettes: gnocchi, fish quenelles (see Chapter 25, page 132), as well as for its sweet version for cream puff pastry shells.

BASIC CREAM PUFF PASTE (*PÂTE À CHOUX*)
(Makes about 2 cups)
Have ready at room temperature

4	**eggs**

In a large saucepan, bring to a boil over medium heat

1 c.	**water**
5 Tbs.	**butter**
¼ tsp.	**salt**

When the butter is melted, remove from heat and add all at once

1 c.	**flour**

Beat rapidly with a sturdy wooden spoon, return to medium heat and continue beating until the mixture thickens and pulls away from the sides of the pan. Remove from heat.

One by one beat in the 4 eggs, making sure each one is absorbed before adding the next. Beat until smooth.

This paste is at its best if used right away. However, when cooled it can be rubbed with butter and stored in the fridge for a few days or in the freezer. To reheat, put it in a saucepan with a little cream and stir over low heat until lukewarm.

NOTE: If you are using the *pâte à choux* for desserts, add 1 tsp. **sugar** to the water mix.

CHEESE CROQUETTES

We used to beg my Swiss mother-in-law to make these for Sunday night supper. In fact, her kitchen artistry was my first exposure to *pâte à choux* and its versatility. She used Gruyère cheese, of course, but you can get away with Parmesan, Romano, or a mixture of other sharp cheeses. It's a great way to use up those annoying scraps.

Following the above recipe, make

2 c.	*pâte à choux*

While still warm, beat in

1 c.	**grated cheese**

Beat until the mixture binds together. Spread on a greased platter and put in fridge until thoroughly chilled.

Proceed according to the instructions in the Basic Croquette Recipe on page 76, which I will repeat here.

Prepare	1 plate	**flour**
	1 shallow dish	1 **egg** beaten with 1 Tbs. of **water** and 1 Tbs. canola **oil**
	1 plate	**bread crumbs**

Start slowly preheating the deep fat oil to **365°** F. Cut the chilled dough into oblongs about 2 inches long. Roll them in the flour; shake off excess flour; dip them into the egg mixture, making sure they're completely coated; finally, roll them in the bread crumbs, making sure the crumbs adhere. If you like, you can repeat the egg and bread crumb maneuver to secure the coating. Work lightly with your fingers, using a spoon to help if necessary. Place the croquettes on a rack to dry for about 15 minutes, if you have time.

When oil temperature reaches **365°** F, deep fry a few at a time, leaving plenty of space for the balls to expand. Keep a close watch on them, as they only take a couple of minutes to reach a golden brown color. Remove with slotted spoon and put on paper towel to absorb excess fat. Keep warm till serving. If you have to reheat them, use a **450°** F oven.

Serve with a **mixed green salad** and a glass of **white wine**. What a delicious light supper!

CHAPTER 15: TURNOVERS

Turnovers are made from rolled-out **biscuit or pie dough** on which a **filling** is piled and then is folded over, sealed and baked in a hot oven. They can be small and used as canapés, medium-sized for a tasty lunch treat, or you can roll out an elongated piece of dough, which you roll up and slice to make pinwheels. The filling is an ideal way to use up cooked meat and vegetables. You can also use store-bought puff pastry or Filo dough for an extra elegant touch.

FILLING for TURNOVERS

Follow the procedure for **Filling for Crêpes** on page 62
or

Make a **brown sauce** (see page 9) and add your minced leftovers
or

Use a **condensed soup**, like tomato or mushroom, to mix your leftovers with.

ASSEMBLING TURNOVERS

Heat oven to **450°** F.
Roll out till thin   **biscuit** or **pie dough**

Cut into 3-inch squares or circles.

Using one of the above suggested fillings, drop by small spoonfuls onto dough squares or circles, leaving a margin, which you moisten. Fold over and press edges together with a fork. Place on baking sheet, brush with melted butter if desired, and bake for about **20 minutes**.

SUGGESTIONS for FILLINGS
- ❖ Meat loaf
- ❖ Minced ham
- ❖ Sausage
- ❖ Corned beef with capers or pickles
- ❖ Fish pieces with hard-boiled eggs and mushrooms
- ❖ Mashed potatoes with sautéed onions or other vegetables

Use Worcester sauce, chili, ketchup, chopped olives, nuts, or anchovies to jazz up your fillings. Let your imagination rule!

FISH TURNOVERS with FILO or PUFF PASTRY DOUGH
(Serves 4)

For the FILLING

Mix together	½ c.	**onions**, chopped
	½ c.	**mushrooms**, chopped, or *Duxelles* (see page 12)
	½ c.	**bread crumbs**
	1	**egg**, beaten
	1 oz. (2 Tbs.)	**melted butter** or **shortening**

Adjust the seasoning with **salt, pepper,** and a pinch of dry or fresh **tarragon** or **herbes de Provence** (optional).

| Mash coarsely | 1 c. | **cooked flounder** or other **fish** (about 2 medium filets) |

Stir into the filling mix.

To ASSEMBLE

Preheat oven to **350°** F.

| Melt | ½ stick (2 oz.) **butter** or **margarine** |

Place on a hard surface

| | 1 sheet | **Filo dough** |

Brush with melted butter. Place a second sheet of dough on top of first sheet and brush with melted butter. Place a mound of filling in middle and fold sides to middle to make a package.

Make more packages by repeating this process with more sheets of Filo dough till all the filling is used up. Put the packages on an ungreased sheet and bake about **25 minutes**.

NOTE: If you find Filo dough too daunting, as I do, try using **puff pastry dough** (*pâte feuilletée*) that you can also find in the supermarket.

VARIATION: An even simpler procedure is to buy **Puff Pastry Shells** and bake them according to the package directions. Let them cool a little and fill them with the filling. Replace the tops and put in the oven again for a few minutes to serve piping hot.

CHAPTER 16: GRATINÉES or SCALLOPED DISHES

This is a wonderful way to recycle cooked potatoes or other vegetables. You can add some cooked meat pieces for variety. All you need to make is a basic béchamel. Pour it over your leftovers nicely arranged in an oven-proof dish, sprinkle on some grated cheese and/or bread crumbs, if desired, and bake it for about half an hour.

BASIC GRATINÉE RECIPE

(Serves 4)

Preheat oven to **375°** F.

Make	1 to 2 c.	**basic béchamel** (2:2:1, see page 8), depending on the quantity of your leftovers. If possible, use **stock**.

Butter an oven-proof dish. Spread **sliced leftovers** on bottom. Sprinkle with **herbs** and minced **garlic**, if desired. Pour on the white sauce.

Sprinkle with **grated cheese**, or with **bread crumbs** dotted with **butter** or **margarine**.

Bake for about **30 minutes**. You can brown it under the broiler for a few minutes if needed.

SUGGESTED COMBINATIONS

- ❖ **Potatoes and ham pieces**. You can sauté sliced **onions** in the shortening when you make the béchamel. Add grated **cheese** to the white sauce or top the dish with grated cheese.
- ❖ **Zucchini** and/or **yellow squash**, with or without **chicken** chunks. Combine with **onions**, as above.
- ❖ **Cauliflower or broccoli**, cut in pieces, covered with a cheese-enhanced béchamel. This is a classic and goes well with cold sliced meat or chicken.
- ❖ **Ham and hard-boiled eggs**. This is extra good if you can add some leftover spinach.

❖ **Pot roast**. Use leftover gravy and stock in the béchamel. Add some **mushrooms**, or *Duxelles* (see page 12) if you have it. Slice thinly and cover with the veggies from the pot.

❖ **Turkey**. Spread leftover **stuffing** on bottom, cover with turkey slices or pieces, and cover with a béchamel which you have combined with leftover **gravy**. You can also scatter the cooked, chopped **giblets** over the turkey slices, as well as some cooked, sliced **mushrooms**.

CHAPTER 17: LOAVES & BIRDS

Meat loaf has been around forever, and you undoubtedly have your favorite combination. But a "loaf" can be made from other ingredients than fresh ground meat. The other night I had a piece of salmon left over and from it made a very respectable fish loaf. A turkey or chicken loaf can be an elegant end to those carcasses.

LOAVES

MEAT LOAF

When you are combining your ground beef with your other favorite ingredients, remember that certain leftovers can be incorporated into the meat mixture. This will add variety and also help stretch the budget. However, be careful not to overdo it. You can mix in a little **rice**, or small chunks of **polenta**. Leftover **tomato sauce** or **mushrooms** are great. Or slice a **hard-boiled egg** and lay it down the middle. Use your imagination, but try not to use more than two leftovers to avoid taste conflicts.

TIP: Line the pan with bacon strips for extra flavor.

Please go to **the FORETASTE, What Makeovers Can I Create for These Leftovers?** (see page xxi). There you will find suggestions for leftover meat loaf.

FISH LOAF
(Serves 2)

Preheat oven to **350°** F.
Grease   **a small loaf pan**

Combine in a bowl

1 c.	**cooked fish**, in small pieces
2	**eggs**
¼ c.	**bread crumbs**
2 Tbs.	**cream** or **half & half**
2 Tbs.	**parsley, cilantro**, or **dill**, chopped
1 Tbs.	**onion**, chopped
1 tsp.	**lemon juice**
Or 1 tsp.	**Dijon mustard**

Stir well and adjust the moisture by adding a little more bread crumbs or cream. Pack the mixture into the loaf pan and bake in oven about 30 minutes.

Serve with a **cucumber sauce** (see page 10).

NOTE: You could add a few capers if using a dill and mustard option.

CHICKEN or TURKEY LOAF
(Serves 4)

Preheat oven to **350° F.**
Grease or line with **bacon** **a medium-sized loaf pan**

Combine in a bowl

2 c.	**cooked chicken** or **turkey** in small pieces
2	**eggs**
¼ to ½ c.	**bread crumbs**
about ¼ c.	**cream** or **half & half**
¼ c.	**parsley**, chopped
2 Tbs.	**onion**, chopped

Adjust the seasoning and moisture according to the leftovers you are incorporating into the loaf. For example, you can add **gravy, cooked giblets, chopped nuts**, etc. Bake for about **30 minutes**.

Serve with a **tomato sauce**.

BIRDS

Birds are thin slices of meat wrapped around a filling and baked or braised. They are an excellent way to stretch a limited supply of (uncooked) meat. For example, you might have a couple of extra raw boneless chicken breasts. Slice them very thin and put a filling of chopped up vegetable leftovers on each slice. Roll them up, place in an ovenproof dish with a sauce on top and bake in a moderate oven. Here is an example.

CHICKEN BREAST BIRDS

(Serves 4)

Preheat oven to **350°** F.

Grease   **an ovenproof dish**

Cut lengthwise into thin slices

2   **raw boneless chicken breasts**

Pound them lightly with a pestle or the bottom of a plate to make them very thin. Put aside.

For the FILLING

Mix together	1 c.	**leftover vegetables**, chopped
	2	**eggs**, beaten
	1 to 2 Tbs.	**bread crumbs**
	2 Tbs.	**celery** and/or **onions**, minced (or *mirepoix*, see page 12)

Adjust the seasoning by adding appropriate **herbs** and checking the salt and pepper. You can also add a tablespoon of minced **ham**, a little grated sharp **cheese**, or some minced **mushrooms** (or ***Duxelles***, see page 12). Make sure the filling is nice and moist.

Spoon some filling on each meat slice, roll it up, making a package, and fasten it with a toothpick. Place in a greased ovenproof dish.

Cover with a **tomato sauce, mushroom sauce**, or any of the appropriate béchamel-based sauces on pages 10 and 11.

Sprinkle with grated cheese and bake for about **30 minutes**.

ALTERNATIVE COOKING METHOD (BRAISED)

When you have assembled your birds, roll them in seasoned flour and sauté them on low heat in **butter** or **olive oil**, turning them as they brown. Add ¼ cup **stock**, **milk**, or **half & half** and flavor with a splash of **white wine**. Cover the skillet and simmer very gently for **20 to 30 minutes**.

SUGGESTIONS

VEAL: The classic birds are **veal** birds, made with pounded veal scaloppini or thin slices of veal roast. If you go this route, be sure the filling is very moist (see recipe above). You can add some chopped **bacon pieces** or **salt pork**. If you cook them on the stovetop, make sure to maintain about ½ inch of liquid on the bottom of the skillet. Veal birds are wonderful with a **mushroom sauce** (see page 11). Use the remainder of the birds' cooking liquid to make the sauce.

TURKEY: If you use slices of raw **turkey**, again, be sure your filling is very moist, and don't let the birds dry out. As a filling, you could use the recipe for stale bread **stuffing** on page 139.

STEAK: If you have a stray uncooked **steak**, you can make birds by slicing the meat very thin and overlapping the strips. After you put on the filling, you will probably need several toothpicks to hold them together, or, better yet, you can tie them with kitchen twine. Brown them over medium heat in **oil** or **bacon fat**, add ½ inch of stock, and simmer over **low heat** for about **an hour**, or until the meat is very tender. Use the remaining liquid to make the sauce.

FISH: A variation on the concept of birds is a **fish roll**. Use thin filets of fish, sole for example, and spread an appropriate filling on ¾ of the surface. Roll it up and fasten with a toothpick. Bake in a **350° F** oven for about **20 minutes**. Rather than bothering about making a filling, you can call on your Mushroom Preparation (see page 99). A **cucumber sauce** (see page 10) goes well with this.

CHAPTER 18: MEATS

BASIC POT PIE RECIPE

With frozen pastry crusts from your arsenal, you can quickly assemble a pot pie with an assortment of leftover **chicken, turkey, meat, or seafood**. If you don't have leftover vegetables, you will need to boil or steam some first.

(Serves 3 to 4)

Thaw	2 frozen	**pie crusts** (or see page 51 for homemade pie crust recipe)

Preheat oven to **400°** F.

Have ready		**a casserole dish** or a **deep pie plate**
Make	2 c.	**béchamel** (2:2:1; see page 8). Use stock appropriate for your leftover meat or seafood.
Mix in	2 c.	**cooked chicken, turkey, ham, meat** or **seafood**, cut into small chunks
	1 to 2 c.	**cooked vegetables**, cut into pieces
	2 Tbs.	**parsley**, chopped
	1 tsp. to 1 Tbs.	**appropriate spices** or **herbs**

Line the casserole dish or deep pie plate with one of the pie crusts. Pour in the above mixture. Cover with second crust, seal edges, and cut slits in top crust. Bake for about **45 minutes**.

Good vegetable additions: **carrots, peas, green beans, broccoli, onions, potatoes, mushrooms.**

VARIATIONS: If you are counting calories, you can dispense with the pie crusts by pouring the hot béchamel mixture into a casserole dish and topping it with blobs of **dumpling dough**. Cover and put in a preheated **375°** F oven for about **20 minutes**. See page 130 for dumpling recipe.

You could also use spoonfuls of **biscuit dough** instead of the pie crust (see recipe below). Bake the béchamel mixture in a **375°** F oven for about **10 minutes** until it is hot and beginning to bubble. Drop spoonfuls of biscuit dough over it and put back in oven for about 12 minutes.

Below is a recipe for drop biscuits if you don't want to use store-bought biscuit dough.

DROP BISCUITS
(from *Joy of Cooking*)

(Makes about small 12 biscuits)

Mix in a bowl	1 c.	**flour**, sifted
	1½ tsp.	**baking powder**
	½ tsp.	**salt**
Pour on	2 ½ Tbs.	**vegetable oil** (not olive)
	⅓ c.	**milk**

Mix with a fork until the dough comes away from the sides of the bowl. Drop by spoonfuls onto the bubbling pot pie mixture in above recipe and bake for about **12 minutes**.

Or you can drop spoonfuls on an ungreased baking sheet and bake at **475°** F for about **10 minutes**.

BEEF PAPRIKA

Beef normally is not very good reheated (better to slice it thin and serve it cold with a salad or in sandwiches with homemade mayo), but here is a handy recipe which is good served over noodles or *spaetzle* (see page 112 for mashed potato *spaetzle*). This would be a great funeral for a roast beef dinner.

(Serves 3-4)

Sauté together lightly in oil and put aside on a plate

	2 to 3 c.	**cooked roast beef** or **steak** cut into ¾-inch cubes
	½ to 1	**onion**, chopped

In same pan, simmer briefly

	2 large	**tomatoes**, peeled, seeded, and chopped
	Or 1 to 1½ c.	**canned tomatoes**

Stir in the meat mix. Cover and simmer for **2 hours**, adding water if necessary.

Stir in	1 to 3 tsp.	**paprika**
	½ c.	**sour cream**

Season with **salt** and **pepper** and serve over noodles, egg dumplings, or *spaetzle*.

MOCK BEEF STROGANOFF

This is one of many dishes in my arsenal of creamed dishes. I call it "mock" because you are supposed to start with fresh beef. However, there is no reason why you can't recycle cooked roast beef, steak, or even chuck roast, provided the meat has not been cooked with tomatoes.

(Serves 4 to 5)

Cut into short, thin strips and set aside

2 c.	**cooked beef** or **steak**

In a large skillet, melt

2 Tbs.	**butter**

Add and sauté gently

¼ c.	**onion**, chopped or thinly sliced

(Optional; delicious, but not authentic)

½ c.	**mushrooms**, sliced

When the mushrooms (if using) are slightly browned, stir in the meat. Set aside.

In a saucepan, melt

	2 Tbs.	**butter**
Add and stir	2 Tbs.	**flour**
(Optional)	1 tsp.	**dry mustard**

Stir until well blended.

Add	1 c.	**strong beef bouillon** (you can use a cube)

Stir vigorously and simmer gently for a few minutes.

Add	½ c.	**sour cream** or *crème fraîche*

Stir until well blended, but do not bring to a boil.

Pour the sauce over the meat mixture and heat through, without boiling. Garnish with chopped **parsley** and serve on a platter surrounded by **rice**.

SHEPHERD'S PIE

Shepherd's pie is one of my favorites. It has infinite possibilities. You can use leftover mashed potatoes and cook a fresh meat mix, or maybe you have some leftover meat loaf that you can crumble on the bottom of an ovenproof dish, or some chili which you can spread on the bottom and top with either fresh or leftover mashed potatoes. The classic recipe calls for ground **lamb**, but **beef**, **pork**, **ham**, or **sausage** will also do. I have even done it with oysters and leftover mashed potatoes. Here are the basic procedures if you have to start either part from scratch.

(Serves 3 to 4)

For the MEAT MIXTURE

Sauté together	1 Tbs.	**butter or oil**
	½ to 1 lb.	**ground fresh meat**
	Or	**chopped cooked meat**
	¼ to ½ c.	**onions**, chopped
	1 or 2 cloves	**garlic**, chopped
	¼ c.	**celery**, chopped
(Optional)	½ c.	**mushrooms**, thinly sliced
Add	pinch	**salt, pepper**
	¼ tsp.	**any appropriate spices** or **herbs**
	2 Tbs.	**parsley**, chopped
Moisten with	¼ c.	**white wine, stock**, or **tomato juice**

You can jazz up this mixture according to your imagination. Try **paprika**, various **peppers**, **cumin**, etc.

For the MASHED POTATOES

In large sauce pan, bring salted water to boil. Peel, cut into cubes, and add

to boiling water	2 to 4	**baking potatoes**
	½ to 1	**onion**, roughly chopped
	1 clove	**garlic**

Boil until soft. Drain well. Put back in sauce pan and allow to dry out a bit over low heat. Mash with masher or beaters.

Beat in	¼ to ½ stick (1 to 2 oz.) **butter or margarine**

Beat until butter is melted and texture is smooth.

Gradually beat in   ½ to1 c.   **hot milk** or **half & half**

You can vary the quantity of butter and milk depending on how creamy you want your mashed potatoes.

To ASSEMBLE the SHEPHERD'S PIE

Preheat oven to **375°** F. Butter a 6- x 10-inch ovenproof dish. Spread cooked meat mix on bottom. Top with mashed potatoes (adding milk or cream if too stiff).

Sprinkle with   **grated Parmesan** or shredded
                                 cheddar cheese (not a good idea if
                                 using with lamb) or **bread crumbs**
Bake in oven **20 to 30 minutes**.

MOUSSAKA, Turkish Style

Moussaka always makes a sensation on a buffet table; its lovely black, shiny mound evokes enthusiastic curiosity. You don't need a lot of leftover lamb to feed a large crowd. You will need a total of four eggplants for this quantity and also two cups of tomato or pasta sauce to accompany it.

(Serves about 16)

STEP 1:
Cut in half lengthwise
                 3   **medium to large eggplants**

Run a knife around the inside of skin. Score pulp deeply.

Heat in skillet   2 Tbs.   **oil** (preferably olive)
Sauté two eggplant halves skin up for a minute.

Add   1 tsp.   **lemon juice**
                    2 Tbs.   **hot water**

Cover and cook **10 minutes** over medium heat. Remove to side dish. Repeat above procedure two more times for the other two eggplants. Scoop out pulp carefully and reserve the whole skins. Mash pulp in large bowl.

STEP 2:

Peel 1 (another) **medium to large eggplant**

(Optional: Save the peel strips. Boil them a few minutes, drain, and use later when lining the mold.)

Cut peeled eggplant into ½ inch crosswise slices.

Put in a paper bag

½ c. **flour**

Add ½ tsp. each **salt** and **pepper**

Put slices in bag and shake well to coat.

Heat in skillet ⅓ c. **oil** (preferably olive)

Sauté eggplant slices gently until lightly browned. Set aside.

STEP 3:

Sauté in large skillet

1 lb. **ground fresh lamb**

Or **chopped cooked lamb**

If using cooked lamb, add it after sautéing the following ingredients. (Using lamb is traditional, but you could make the moussaka with ground beef or without any meat, for a vegetarian version.)

Add and sauté ½ c. **mushrooms**, chopped

2 cloves **garlic**, chopped

½ **medium onion**, chopped

Add 1 **14.5-oz. can of tomatoes**

Stir these ingredients well. Correct the seasoning by adding about a Tbs. **salt** and ½ tsp. **pepper**. Add some **herbes de Provence**, or any combination of **oregano**, **basil**, **thyme**, **rosemary**. Go heavy on the rosemary if using lamb, but chop it fine.

Stir contents of skillet into the eggplant pulp in the large bowl (from Step 1).

In a small bowl beat slightly

2 **eggs**

Stir them into the pulp mix.

Stir into mix   2 Tbs.   **parsley**, chopped
If this mixture seems too runny, you can add
                2 to 3 Tbs.   **bread crumbs**

STEP 4:

Heat oven to **375°** F. Place a pan of water in it to heat.

Generously oil a **charlotte mold** or **Pyrex bowl**. Line the sides with the reserved skins (from Step 1) with the black skin facing out. Fill in the gaps with the boiled strips (from Step 2) if necessary. Fill the mold with layers of pulp mix and sautéed slices, finishing with a layer of slices (probably three layers of each: first pulp mix, then slices, etc.) Fold any over-hanging skins back over the mixture. This almost makes a kind of package.

Place mold or bowl in the pan of hot water in oven. Bake for about **1½ hours**. Remove and let stand about 30 minutes for it to set.

Unmold onto an ovenproof dish. Make sure the concoction slithers around in the mold before you attempt to reverse it.

Serve hot with tomato sauce (see page 11 or 14).

NOTE: This dish is best if made at least a day ahead of time. You can let it stand on the counter or on a cool porch for 24 hours. If you wait 2 or 3 days, you will need to keep it in the fridge. Reheat it in a slow oven. If you have made a meatless version, you can serve it at room temperature.

MEAT PATTIES and MEAT BALLS

You can stretch your supply of **ground beef** by incorporating a little leftover **mashed potato, dumplings,** or **stale bread**. Be careful not to overdo these added ingredients. Mash them in a bowl; add an **egg**, some minced **onion** and **garlic**, a sprinkling of **herbs** to your liking. Then beat in the ground meat and knead with your hands to form patties or balls. If you like, you can roll them in **bread crumbs**.

Patties are best sautéed. Meat balls can be sautéed or simmered in stock. Use the stock to make sauce.

CHICKEN and EGGPLANT PARMESAN
(Serves 2 to 3)

Preheat oven to **375°** F.

Peel and cut crosswise into half-inch slices

| 1 | **large eggplant** |

Put the slices in a plastic colander and sprinkle with **salt**. Let them drain for a half to one hour. Press dry with paper towels.

In a large skillet heat

| 2 Tbs. | **olive oil** (or 1 Tbs. each of olive and canola oil) |

Cover the pan and sauté the eggplant slices on both sides over low heat. You may need to add a little more oil if the slices become too dry. But be careful, because the slices will give back later the oil they absorbed, and you might end up with a greasy product. When they are lightly browned and fairly soft, remove them to a plate.

While the eggplant is cooking, make about

| 1 c. | **medium béchamel** (see page 8) |

For extra flavor, chop and sauté in the béchamel butter or shortening

| ¼ c. | **combination of onions**, **carrots**, **celery**, **mushrooms**, and **garlic** |

Part of the béchamel liquid should be **canned tomatoes** with their juice

| (Optional) Add | 1 Tbs. | **red wine** |
| Add | 1 c. | **cooked chicken pieces** |

Grease an ovenproof dish and place half the eggplant slices on the bottom. Cover with one half of the sauce. Continue with a layer of the rest of the eggplant, followed by the rest of the sauce. Sprinkle grated Parmesan cheese over the top, cover with foil, and bake for about ½ hour. Remove the foil and sprinkle with 1 to 2 Tbs. water if the mixture seems dry. Bake another **15 minutes**.

Serve with rice or, better yet, some fried polenta (see pages 119 and 120).

NOTE: If you have enough leftover **chicken gravy**, by all means use it instead of the béchamel. Jazz it up with some sautéed **onions**, etc. as per above. But be sure to add some **tomatoes**, freshly chopped or canned.

BASIC CHILI RECIPE

(Serves 4)

Chili can be a wonderful catch-all way of using up various odds and ends of meat, chicken, or turkey. A simple, spicy tomato sauce is made in a large skillet and combined with cooked dried beans and ground meat. Here is a basic procedure to get you started.

In a large skillet, heat

	2 Tbs.	**olive oil**
Add and sauté till wilted		
	½	**onion**, chopped
	¼ to ½	**carrot**, chopped
	3 cloves	**garlic**, chopped
	½	**bell pepper**, seeded and chopped
(Optional)	½	**chili pepper**, or other hot pepper, seeded and finely chopped
Season with any of the following		
	1 tsp.	**cumin**
	about 1 Tbs.	**chili powder** (if you haven't used fresh chili)
	1 large	**bay leaf**
	pinches	**dried oregano, thyme, basil**
	Or 1 Tbs.	**herbes de Provence**
Add	1	14-oz. **can diced tomatoes**
(Optional)	½ c.	**red wine**
Or (optional)	1 c.	**beer**

Simmer for about **15 minutes**.

Add	1 to 1½ c.	**cooked meat, chicken, turkey**, or **meat loaf**, chopped

Simmer for another **15 minutes**.

Add	1	14-oz. **can kidney or white beans**
	Or 2 c.	**dried beans, home cooked**
If too dry, add	1 to 2 Tbs.	**stock**

Simmer about **45 minutes**. Chili will pick up flavor if you let it stand, even overnight.

See page 131 to serve it with dumplings.

CHAPTER 19: CURRIES

Curry is a very special way to enhance cut-up cooked meat or chicken or hard-boiled eggs. A dash of it can also be added to soups, rice dishes, the béchamel for vegetable gratinée dishes, salads. It goes wonderfully with lamb or chicken. Here is a basic procedure to use up pieces of cooked chicken, turkey, or meat. If you are using up a leg of lamb, don't forget to scoop the marrow out of the bones and add it to the sauce.

BASIC PROCEDURE for MEAT CURRY
(Serves 3 to 4)

Cut into 1-inch chunks

2 to 3 c.	**cooked chicken**, **turkey**, **duck**, **beef**, **lamb**, or **pork**

Put about 2 Tbs. **flour** into a paper bag, add the meat pieces, and shake to coat them with the flour.

In a saucepan, heat   4 Tbs.   **oil** or **butter**
Add the floured meat chunks and brown them gently on all sides. Remove to a plate.*****

In the remaining oil, sauté slowly

	½ c.	**onions**, chopped
	¼ c.	**celery**, chopped
	¼ c.	**carrots**, chopped
	1 large	**apple**, peeled and cut into large chunks
	1 large clove	**garlic**, mashed
When lightly browned, add		
	2 to 3 tsp.	**curry** powder (add more if you like)
(Optional)	1 tsp.	**powdered ginger**

Sprinkle with flour left over from paper bag.
Stir gently and add

	2 to 3 c.	**stock** (chicken or beef bouillon cubes OK)
Add	any leftover	**gravy** or **meat juice**
(Optional)	¼ c.	**raisins** or **currants**

Bring to simmer. Add the reserved meat chunks. Cover and simmer on very low heat about ½ **hour**.

Best if made several hours or a day ahead.
Serve with boiled or steamed rice.

* This procedure should be used only if the chunks of meat are large and relatively juicy. Otherwise, omit and just add smaller pieces of meat to the simmering vegetable and stock mix.

NOTE: For the liquid, you can substitute **canned tomato** chunks for some or all of the stock, but in this case, omit the apple.

SIMPLE PROCEDURE for CURRY CREAM SAUCE

Make a **brown sauce** (see page 9), adding 1 to 2 Tbs. **curry powder** to the sautéed vegetable mix (or *mirepoix*). Simmer covered (or uncovered if too liquid) for ½ **hour**. Add **raisins** if you like. Best served with boiled or steamed **rice**.

SUGGESTIONS

❖ This is a good cream sauce for **eggs or vegetables**. You can make it creamier by making a basic béchamel (see page 8) instead of a brown sauce. Simmer chopped onions and garlic (optional) in the shortening and blend in 1 to 2 Tbs. curry before adding the flour and the liquid. You can use milk if you like and enrich it with ¼ c. cream or half & half. Leave out the raisins.

❖ A curry cream sauce is delicious over pieces of cooked **fish**, especially if you sauté sliced **mushrooms** with the onion mix. You need only to simmer the sauce about 10 minutes. Pour it over the fish and brown it for about 10 minutes in a hot oven.

❖ This would be a different kind of end to the **holiday turkey**. Follow the Basic Procedure for a Meat Curry above, or incorporate chunks of turkey into the Curry Cream Sauce. Add the cooked **giblets**, if desired.

CHAPTER 20: VEGETABLES

Cooked vegetables can be reincarnated in many different forms. Incorporating them into a béchamel for a creamed vegetable dish is a simple solution. An example follows, using corn. They can also be mixed into stuffed vegetable casings, along with cooked meat, ham, or seafood. They can be made into puddings, which are closely related to the timbales in Chapter 11, page 57. Also, please see Gratinées, Chapter 16, page 81. Many other vegetarian dishes can be used as a vehicle to incorporate a few pieces of cooked meat or chicken. The recipe for Eggplant & Zucchini Crustless Pie (see page 103) is an example.

CREAMED VEGETABLE DISHES

CREAMED CORN

You will be making a standard béchamel (see page 8), the amount depending on how much cut corn you have on hand. You will need 1 cup béchamel for every 1 to 1½ cup cut corn.

(Serves 3-5)

In a saucepan, melt

	2 to 4 Tbs.	**butter**, depending on how much béchamel you are making
Sauté gently	½ medium	**onion**, chopped
	½ stalk	**celery**, chopped
Stir in	2 to 4 Tbs.	**flour**
Add and stir	1 to 2 c.	**milk** or **stock**
Fold in	1 to 2 c.	**cut cooked corn** (from 2 to 4 cobs)
	1 Tbs.	**parsley**, chopped
(Optional)	¼ tsp.	**cumin**

Simmer gently for **20 to 30 minutes**.

SUGGESTIONS

❖ Add chopped **green** or **red pepper** to the sauté mix.
❖ You can also coarsely purée the corn for a smoother texture.

CREAMED CAULIFLOWER in MUSTARD or CHEESE SAUCE

Follow the procedure above for creamed corn, omitting the cumin. Instead, incorporate 1 Tbs. **Dijon mustard** or ½ cup grated **cheddar cheese**. Gently fold in cauliflower pieces and barely simmer for about **10 minutes**.

MUSHROOM PREPARATION

Mushrooms are a great resource to add depth to creamed dishes, sauces, and any vegetable or meat mixture. The following procedure can be prepared ahead of time and stored in the refrigerator, handy for use at a moment's notice. It is a variation on the *Duxelles* recipe on page 12. Add it to any of these vegetable dishes, if you like.

Chop **mushrooms** coarsely, mix with chopped **onions** and **garlic**, and simmer in **olive oil** or **butter** uncovered for about **20 minutes**. Hold off on salt, pepper, and spices, as you might not know exactly where this mix will be used.

BAKED STUFFED VEGETABLES

Vegetable casings make good containers for ground-up leftovers, such as meat, sausage, chicken, vegetables, and rice or corn. If you have a little leftover rice or couscous, you can stretch the stuffing ingredients by adding it.

Sometimes partially cooked before being stuffed, the stuffed shells are baked from ½ to 1 hour. Served with a simple green salad, they make a nutritious light meal. You can let your imagination run wild as you combine the ingredients for the stuffing.

The stuffed casings can also be accompanied by almost any sauce. Plain yogurt is especially good. Best vegetables to stuff: zucchini, eggplant, green peppers. I have also added a friend's recipe for stuffed avocados.

BASIC PROCEDURE for BAKED STUFFED VEGETABLE CASINGS

(Serves 4)

For the CASINGS

Wash and cut lengthwise

> 4 medium or 2 large **zucchini**
> *Or* 2 medium **eggplants**

Scoop out contents, chop finely, and put in a bowl. However, if the seeds are large, discard them.

Simmer the casings 3 minutes in

> 1 to 1½ c. **bouillon** (cubes or stock)

Dip quickly in cold water to stop cooking process and preserve color. Reserve the stock.

For the STUFFING

Add to the chopped vegetable flesh in the bowl

> 1 c. **leftover meat**, **sausage**, **chicken**, or **seafood**, chopped fine
> ¼ c. **onion**, minced
> 1 Tbs. **garlic**, **chopped**
> 1 Tbs. **celery**, chopped
> 1 tsp. **parsley**, **herbs**, **cilantro**, or any other appropriate **seasonings**, chopped

Place casings in greased baking pan. Fill with the stuffing. Sprinkle with **bread crumbs** or **grated cheese** or both. Dot with **butter** or sprinkle with **olive oil**. Pour a little water on the bottom of the baking pan. Bake for about **½ hour** at **350° F**.

To serve, you can make a standard **béchamel** (2:2:1; see page 8) with the stock and some cream, to which you can add tomato paste or sauce, and pour it over as a sauce. As mentioned above, plain **yogurt** is good, especially if it is enhanced with a little chopped **mint** when the stuffing is made with lamb.

BAKED STUFFED PEPPERS or TOMATOES

Preheat oven to **350°** F.

Cut the tops off **green peppers** or **large tomatoes**
Reserve the tops.

Scoop out the seeds of the peppers or the flesh and seeds of the tomatoes. (Reserve the tomato flesh for later use in a sauce or stew.)
Grease the outside of the casings and fill with stuffing (see above recipe). Put the tops back on.

Place in a greased ovenproof dish and pour a little water on the bottom of the dish.

For the peppers, bake about **50 minutes**, for the tomatoes, about **30 minutes**.

RAE'S BAKED STUFFED AVOCADOS
(Serves 4)

Preheat oven to **375°** F.

Peel, cut in half lengthwise
2 large **avocados** (not Haas)

Discard the stones and sprinkle lightly with salt.
Place avocado halves hollow side up in a greased baking dish.

Make	1 c.	**semi-thick béchamel** (2½:2½:1; see Filling for Crêpes, page 62). Use some **white wine** with it.
Stir in	¼ c.	mild **grated cheese**
	Or 2 oz.	**cream cheese**
Add	½ to 1 c.	**cooked shrimp, chicken, turkey,** or **ham**, chopped

Check the seasoning. The flavor should be pronounced to counteract the blandness of the avocado.

Pour mixture into hollows of avocado halves and sprinkle on some **grated cheese**. Bake for about **30 minutes** until bubbling and browned.

BAKED STUFFED EGGPLANT SHELLS, VEGETARIAN

Partially roasting the eggplant before stuffing imparts an extra succulent flavor.

(Serves 4 to 6)

Preheat oven to **350°** F.

Cut in half lengthwise

> 2 large or 4 small **eggplants**

Place them cut side down in an oven-proof dish greased with **olive oil**. Bake them for about **30 minutes**. The insides should be soft but not mushy. Run a knife around the inside of the skin and scoop out the insides. Chop them coarsely and put aside.

Sauté lightly in olive oil

	½	**onion**, chopped
	2 cloves	**garlic**, chopped
(Optional)	½ stalk	**celery**, chopped
(Optional)	½	**carrot**, chopped fine

When wilted, add

	½ c.	**canned tomatoes**
	the chopped	**eggplant flesh**
		some herbs of your choice: **basil, rosemary, parsley, herbes de Provence**
	pinch	**salt** and **pepper**
(Optional)	1 tsp.	**lemon juice**
(Optional)	2 Tbs.	**feta, ricotta,** or **grated Parmesan cheese**

Simmer this mixture a few minutes. If you have some leftover **rice**, you can add it, or **bread crumbs** if the mixture is too liquid.

Fill the eggplant shells with this mixture. Sprinkle with **grated cheese** and 1 to 2 Tbs. **olive oil**.

Put under medium broiler until crisp and brown.

EGGPLANT & ZUCCHINI CRUSTLESS PIE

This dish can serve as an accompaniment to meat or chicken, or if you add cooked meat or chicken pieces, it can stand alone as a light lunch or supper, with a green salad.

(Serves 2 to 4)

Preheat oven to **375° F.**

Grease a baking sheet with 1 Tbs. **olive** or **canola oil**.

Peel and cut lengthwise into half-inch slices

1 large	**eggplant**

Cut into lengthwise slices

	1 medium	**zucchini**
(Optional)	1 to 2 small	**yellow summer squash**

Place slices on the baking sheet, turning them so that both sides are coated with oil. Salt them very lightly. Bake **30 to 40 minutes**, turning them once.

Meanwhile, chop finely, mix, and put aside

½	**onion**
3 to 4 cloves	**garlic**
several sprigs	**parsley**, including stems
½ stalk	**celery**

Have on hand	8 oz.	**ricotta cheese**
	1½ c.	**tomato sauce** of your choice (see page 11 or 14 if you want to make your own)

Remove the vegetable slices from oven when they are lightly browned.

Place one half of the mixed slices in a layer in a greased Pyrex pie dish. (Don't use metal with eggplant.) Sprinkle with half the onion mix. Cover with half the ricotta and half the tomato sauce. Continue with the top layer of slices, the rest of the onion mix, ricotta, and tomato sauce. Sprinkle with some **grated cheese**. Put in oven for **45 to 60 minutes**. Best if you let stand at a cool room temperature for 24 hours. Reheat to lukewarm.

NOTE: You can chop about ½ c. **cooked meat or chicken** and spread it on top of the first layer of tomato sauce.

VEGETABLE PUDDINGS

SPINACH or VEGETABLE PUDDING

This is a streamlined way to use up vegetable leftovers.

(Serves 2-3)

Beat	2	**eggs**
Add and mix	1¼ c.	**cooked spinach** or **other vegetables,** chopped
	1 c.	**cottage cheese**
	⅓ c.	**Parmesan cheese**, grated
	1 tsp.	**salt**

Pour mixture into a greased baking dish. Bake at **350°** F for about **30 minutes**.

SOUTHERN CORN PUDDING

This is a vegetable pudding, but it's sweet. It's super simple and very tasty and goes well with ham.

(Serves 4 to 6)

Preheat oven to **350°** F.

Beat together	1 c.	**milk**
	½ c.	**sugar**
	2	**eggs**
	1 stick (4 oz.)	**melted butter** or **margarine**
Sir in	2 c.	**cut cooked corn** (from 4 to 5 cobs)

Spread mixture in a greased ovenproof dish and bake till brown and set, about **30 to 40 minutes**.

CREAMED CORN PUDDING

This pudding is a good accompaniment to a roast chicken or meat.

(Serves 5)

Preheat oven to **425°** F.

Grease **an ovenproof dish**

In blender, pulse until creamy

2 c. **cut cooked corn** (from 4 to 5 cobs)

Set aside in a bowl.

In a skillet, melt 2 Tbs. **butter** or **margarine**

Add and sauté gently over low heat till wilted but not brown

1 c. **onions**, chopped

½ c. **celery**, chopped

Or 1 c. **mirepoix** (see page 12)

Add this mixture to the corn. Season with **salt** and **pepper**.

In a large bowl, beat for 2 minutes

2 **egg yolks**

Stir in the corn and onion/celery mixture.

Mix in ¼ c. **sour cream**

Beat until stiff 2 **egg whites**

Fold them into the corn mixture.

Pour mixture into greased ovenproof dish and bake for **15 minutes**. Then turn down heat to **350°** F and bake for about **30 minutes** more. Let rest about 10 minutes before serving.

———————

CORN PUDDING

This recipe is similar to one for a soufflé, except that it uses a lighter béchamel and fewer eggs.

(Serves 5)

Preheat oven to **350°** F.

Make in a large sauce pan

	1 c.	**medium béchamel** (2:2:1; see page 8)
Add	2 c.	**cut cooked corn** (from 4 to 5 cobs)
(Optional)	¼ c.	**bell pepper**, chopped or some **piemento**
(Optional)	½ tsp.	**cumin**

Separate into two bowls

	2	**eggs**

Pour some of the hot corn mixture into the egg yolks and beat well. Return this to the sauce pan, mix well and bring almost to a simmer for a couple of minutes. Do not boil.

Beat the egg whites till stiff and fold into the corn mixture. Pour mixture into greased baking dish and bake for about **30 minutes**.

NOTE: You can sprinkle the greased ovenproof dish with **bread crumbs** or **grated cheese**, and you can also put some **minced ham** or **crisp bacon bits** on the bottom.

————————

CHAPTER 21: STIR-FRY

Stir-fry is a quick and super-easy way to recycle **cooked meats**, but the vegetables should be cooked fresh. Sesame seed oil and an Asian sauce of your choice dress up the result.

BASIC STIR-FRY PROCEDURE

From your arsenal   **A wok** or **large skillet**

Cut into thin strips

	assorted	**fresh vegetables** (carrots, celery, broccoli, onions, garlic, etc.)
		cooked meat (pork, beef, chicken, lamb, seafood, etc.)
Have ready	1 tsp.	**grated ginger**

In a wok or frying pan, heat over medium heat

                1 to 2 Tbs.   **canola** or **vegetable oil**

Stir in the vegetables and cook **3 to 4 minutes** till they are softened.

Add   1 Tbs.   **sesame seed oil**

Add the meat and grated ginger, and stir another minute or two. Sprinkle with **rice vinegar**, if desired. Mix in a dollop of **Asian sauce**.

Serve with boiled or steamed white or brown rice.

STIR-FRIED GREENS with BACON

Normally we might throw out the outer leaves of iceberg lettuce, the green ends of leeks, or the leaves that come with a bunch of beets. But wait! All this is nutritious and delicious and will make a tasty and economical meal. Here's how.

(Serves 3 to 4)

Wash in at least 2 waters   **greens from 3 beets**
                                      greens from 2 to 3 leeks
                                      outer leaves of 1 iceberg lettuce

For the beet greens, tear the green part away from the whole length of the red spine. For the leek greens, choose the less tough leaves. Save the tough ones for soup (see pages 23-25).

Spin dry and cut into shreds, cutting the leeks especially fine. Remove to a big bowl.

Cut into 1½-inch pieces
| | ½ lb. | **bacon strips**, or use chunk bacon |

In a wok or large skillet over medium heat, fry the bacon pieces till some of the fat is rendered.

| Add | ½ c. | **onions** or **greens of scallions**, shredded |

Sauté gently till bacon starts to become crisp and onions are slightly brown. If you have a little **hamburger meat** or chopped **ham** on hand, you can add that and sauté it 1 to 2 minutes.

| Add | 2 cloves | **garlic**, finely chopped |

Sauté another minute.

| (Optional) Add | 1 Tbs. | **sesame seed oil** |

Turn up heat to medium high and dump in all the shredded greens. Keep stirring till the greens are cooked through (**2 to 3 minutes**). Taste for seasoning and add **salt**, **pepper**, a dash of **rice vinegar**, some **lemon juice**, or even a few pieces of leftover **tomatoes** (no lemon juice in that case). Stir another minute.

If you want to serve over pasta as a main dish (especially if you have added a little meat or ham), you can stir in ¼ cup **half & half** or **stock**.

———————————

CHAPTER 22: POTATOES

Leftover potatoes are a challenge; so much so that they are usually chucked. But frugality and ingenuity command that you transform them into lovely new dishes. The mashed potato dishes are especially good. Mashed potatoes can be used as a base in croquette recipes (see Chapter 14, page 76, NOTE). Boiled or steamed potatoes can be dressed up in a gratinée (see Chapter 16 page 81), or converted into hash browns. They can also be incorporated into a salad (see Chapter 5, page 37). For more suggestions, please refer to the Foretaste Interactive Guide on page xxi. Not even day-old baked potatoes need go to waste.

POTATO CAKES (Made with mashed potatoes)

This is a great way to use up mashed potatoes.

Mix together   1 to 1½ c.   **leftover mashed potatoes**
                   1 beaten   **egg**
With any of these **celery**, **onions**, **parsley**, **chives**, finely chopped, or grated **nutmeg**. Adjust the seasoning, adding **salt** and **pepper** if necessary.
Shape into balls and flatten.

Dip into a plate of   **bread crumbs, crushed cornflakes**, or **flour**.

In a skillet, brown both sides in   **butter** or **vegetable oil**.

NOTE: You can add **ground ham** and/or **grated cheese** to the potato mix.

POTATO CAKES (Made with cold boiled potatoes)

Follow the above procedure, substituting grated cold boiled potatoes for the mashed potatoes. Make sure the potatoes are very cold, and grate on the largest holes of your box grater. You can leave the skin on if you like.

If you would like to make your cakes more like pancakes, add a little **milk** or **half & half** to make a semi-fluid batter. Brown the cakes in butter over medium heat.

FISH CAKES (Made with mashed potatoes)

This is a good way to use up mashed potatoes and some scraps of yesterday's fish.

In a bowl mix an even proportion of **mashed potatoes** and flaked, **cooked fish**. Add some minced **onions** and a tiny bit of minced **celery**. Beat in 1 to 2 **eggs**, depending on the quantity of your fish/potato mix. Season with **salt** and **pepper**, and add a dash of **curry**, if desired.

Shape mixture into cakes and coat with **bread crumbs**. Sauté cakes in butter over medium heat till nice and brown. Serve with a creamy tomato sauce or a caper sauce (see page 11).

_____

STUFFED BAKED POTATOES

There's nothing more depressing than a soggy, leftover baked potato. But don't despair. Scoop out the flesh, mash it and combine with an **egg**, some **cream**, **minced onion**, **grated cheese**, or ingredients of your imagination. **Minced ham** is nice. You can also do chopped **shrimp**, with a dash of **curry**. Spoon the mixture back into the casings, put in a greased oven-proof dish and bake for about **20 minutes** at **375°** F.

_____

CHANTILLY POTATO CUPS

When you see the word "Chantilly," think whipped cream, but in this case unsweetened. So I'm afraid Reddi-wip won't do. However, this is an elegant way to recycle mashed potatoes. The only ingredient outside of your basic arsenal is the whipping cream.

(Serves 5 to 6)

Preheat oven to **350°** F.

Grease   **5 to 6 ramekins**

Separate into 2 bowls

      1   **egg**

In the yolk bowl, add and beat

     2 c.   **mashed potatoes**

Melt in a skillet and simmer over low heat

	2 Tbs.	**butter**
	2 Tbs.	**onion**, chopped
(Optional)	¼ c.	**bell pepper**, chopped

Add to potato mixture. Adjust the seasoning. Spoon into the greased ramekins, filling about three quarters. Wipe out the bowl.

In this bowl, beat until stiff

	½ c.	**whipping cream**

In another bowl, beat until stiff

		the egg white
Combine with	¼ c.	**grated cheese**

Fold contents of these two bowls together gently and spoon over the potato mixture in the ramekins. Bake for about **30 minutes**.

MOCK POTATO SOUFFLÉ

(Serves 4)

Preheat oven to **325° F.**

Grease		**an ovenproof dish**
Separate	3	**eggs**

Mix together and heat in microwave

	3 c.	**mashed potatoes**
	½ c.	**half & half**
	2 Tbs.	**butter**
Beat them together with		**the 3 egg yolks**
Season with		**salt** and **pepper** or **paprika**

Spread mixture in greased ovenproof dish.

Beat until stiff		**the 3 egg whites** (add one or two more if available)
	¼ tsp.	**salt**
Fold in	⅓ c.	**grated cheese** (Parmcsan best)

Spread this over the potato mixture and bake for **20 to 30 minutes**

111

POTATO *SPAETZLE* or DUMPLINGS

This is a simple way to use up baked or mashed potatoes. You can spread the *spaetzle* in a buttered baking dish, sprinkle them with breadcrumbs and melted butter and brown them under the broiler, or you can use them as an accompaniment to boiled meat dishes (see Beef Paprika, page 88). They're also good just served in reheated gravy, topped with a little grated cheese.

(Makes about 20 small dumplings)

Using MASHED POTATOES

Beat together	2 c.	**mashed potatoes**
	2	**eggs**
	½ c.	**flour**
	1 tsp.	**salt**

This batter should be stiff. If too moist, add a little more flour.

Drop teaspoons of this batter into **gently boiling salted water**. Do not overcrowd. Simmer for about **10 minutes**. Remove with a slotted spoon to a paper towel and cover to keep warm.

Using BAKED or BOILED POTATOES

Make sure the potatoes are very cold. Grate the flesh (no skin) or put it through a ricer.

Follow the above recipe. You will be able to make one-inch balls of the dough, which you will simmer, as above.

REGULAR HASH BROWNS

These are an all-time favorite, and *so* simple to make.

(Serves 3 to 4)

Chop into very small cubes

	4 large	**cold boiled potatoes**

Leave the skin on for extra flavor. Put aside.

In a skillet, heat on low

	1 to 2 Tbs.	**oil** and **butter**
Add and cook until barely wilted		**an onion**, chopped

(Optional)   ½   **bell pepper**, finely chopped

Turn up the heat to medium-high and add the cubed potatoes. Sauté for a few minutes, stirring often with a spatula. Season with **salt and pepper**.

Before serving, sprinkle with some **chopped parsley**.

VARIATION: Cut up some slices of **bacon** and sauté the pieces lightly before adding the onions.

––––––––––––

HASH BROWNS, SWISS STYLE (a.k.a. *ROESTI*)

For this variation, you have to use cold, day-old boiled potatoes. Peel them, grate them coarsely, and put them aside while you go on with the recipe.

(Serves 3 to 4)

Cut into small pieces and fry lightly in a large skillet

	2 to 3 slices	**bacon**, cut into small pieces

Add and fry till slightly browned

	½ medium	**onion**, chopped

Add and melt	2 Tbs.	**butter**
Add	1 lb. (2 c.)	**potatoes**, cooked, cold, peeled, and grated

Press down on the mixture so that it fills the bottom of the skillet and makes a large, flat pancake. Sprinkle lightly with **salt and pepper**. Fry over medium heat for about **15 minutes**.

Invert the pancake onto a plate and slide it back into skillet. Sprinkle with a little **salt and pepper** and cook about **another 15 minutes**.

Cut into wedges while still in the pan.

––––––––––––

CHAPTER 23: PASTAS

Pastas are so soothing and lend themselves so easily to using up leftover meats, seafood, or vegetables that you've probably already been doing this forever. Make a light **béchamel** (1½:1½:1; see page 8) with milk, stock, and/or cream. Season it according to your leftovers, which you will add to the sauce and serve with your favorite freshly-boiled pasta. Last night I had a cooked chicken breast on my hands, so this is what I did.

CHICKEN CHUNKS over PASTA
(Serves 2)

Cut into chunks		**a chicken breast** (or any part of a cooked chicken)
	1 slice	**country ham** (any ham or cooked **bacon**)
Sauté gently together		
	1 Tbs.	**olive oil**
	½	**onion**, chopped
	1 Tbs.	**garlic**, chopped
Add the ham and chicken.		
Sprinkle with	1 to 2 Tbs.	**flour**
Add	1 to 2 c.	combined **stock** and **tomato sauce**
	1 Tbs.	**parsley**, chopped
	¼ c.	**cream** or **half &half**
(Optional)	¼ c.	**white wine**

You can jazz up the sauce with **herbes de Provence**, **oregano**, or **thyme**. I sometimes stretch the sauce with some leftover turkey or chicken stock.
Simmer gently for about **20 minutes**.
Serve with your favorite boiled pasta. (Whole wheat pasta works well.) Top with **grated cheese**.

SUGGESTIONS

- ❖ **Vegetables:** tomatoes, zucchini, broccoli, leeks, chard, asparagus. Use cream for your white sauce, not tomato sauce.
- ❖ **Seafood:** I prefer a cream sauce, maybe with just a little tomato paste added. Add chopped mushrooms for extra flavor.
- ❖ The list goes on and on. This is really one of the simplest and speediest ways to use up pieces of leftover meat or poultry, and the beauty of it is that it will feed a crowd. The combinations are infinite!

STUFFED MANICOTTI

A bubbling dish of manicotti is so attractive. Large tubes of pasta are stuffed with a filling, laid side by side in a shallow dish, and topped with a sauce, usually tomato. The easiest way is to buy a package of manicotti, boil them up, and stuff them. You can also use thin pancakes or crêpes instead of the dry tubes in the commercial package. In this case, follow the instructions for Stuffed Crêpes on page 61.

For the filling, you will be making a thick béchamel (3:3:1; see page 8) and adding your chopped leftovers, enhanced with some herbs. For the sauce, you can make your own tomato sauce (see pages 11 and 14) or use a store-bought variety. Here is one example.

MANICOTTI STUFFED with CHICKEN and ASPARAGUS
(Serves 4)

For the PASTA

Following the instructions on the package, boil until just tender (about **8 minutes**)

8	**manicotti tubes**

Drain, rinse, and remove them to a plate, keeping them separate. Meanwhile, prepare the filling.

For the FILLING

Warm in microwave

1 c.	**chicken stock** or a mix of stock and **cream**

Put aside.

In a saucepan over medium heat, melt

3 Tbs.	**butter** or **shortening**

Add and simmer till wilted

	½	**onion**, chopped fine
	1 Tbs.	**celery**, finely chopped
	1 to 2 cloves	**garlic**, chopped
(Optional)	½ c.	**mushrooms**, chopped
Stir in	3 Tbs.	**flour**

When blended, add the warmed stock and/or cream. Keep stirring till the mixture thickens. Cook on low heat **5 to 10 minutes**.

Stir in	about 1 c.	**cooked chicken** pieces
	about ½ c.	**cooked asparagus**, chopped
	¼ c.	**grated Parmesan cheese**
	1 Tbs.	**parsley**, chopped
Cool slightly and add		
	1	**egg white**

Blend these ingredients well.

To ASSEMBLE

Preheat oven to **375°** F.

Heat in microwave
about 3 c. **tomato sauce** or **light béchamel**
You can use store-bought **Alfredo** or **tomato sauce**, or see pages pages 11 and 14 to make your own.

Spread about a third of it on the bottom of a greased oven-proof dish. With a teaspoon stuff the manicotti with the filling and lay them side by side on top of the sauce. Cover with the rest of the sauce.

Sprinkle with ½ c. **grated Parmesan cheese**
Bake for about **25 minutes**. You can switch to broil for **another 5 to 10 minutes** for a brown and crusty top.

———————————

MANICOTTI STUFFED with FISH

This is a delicious way to stretch a bit of leftover fish or seafood. Chances are that there will be a little sauce left over with it. Scrape it off the fish and reserve it for the sauce.

(Serves 2 to 4)

For the SHELLS and STUFFING

Preheat oven to **375°** F.

Cook according to package instructions

	4	**manicotti shells**

Drain, rinse and put aside.

In a bowl, mix	1 c.	**cooked flaked fish** or **seafood**
	1	**hard-boiled egg**, chopped
	2 oz.	**cream cheese**, mashed
	1 Tbs.	**onion**, minced
	1 Tbs.	**celery**, minced
(Optional)	¼ c.	**mushrooms**, chopped and sautéed, or use *Duxelles* (see page 12)

Stuff the manicotti shells loosely with this mixture. Place in greased ovenproof dish. Cover with the following sauce.

For the SAUCE

Scrape together any leftover fish sauce. Mix in bowl with some **tomato sauce**, **heavy cream**, and/or any leftover **mayonnaise-type sauce**. Add some chopped **dill** or **cilantro**, if desired. This is really a free-lance sauce and can be as fanciful as you please. You can moisten it with some **stock** if necessary. Be sure to make plenty to smother the manicotti. Sprinkle lightly with **grated Parmesan** cheese, dribble some **olive oil** over each manicotti, and place in the upper part of the oven for about **20 minutes**. Brown them off under the broiler for a few minutes if necessary.

NOTE: If you don't have any leftover sauce to work with, make a light **béchamel** (1½:1½:1), using appropriate stock or cream. Add the tomato sauce and the other appropriate recommended ingredients.

LASAGNA

There are more ways to make lasagna than you can count. You probably have your favorite recipe. The nice thing about this all-around dish is that you can incorporate all sorts of leftover meat or vegetables. Think about them when you make the tomato sauce: add some leftover veggies (e.g. **corn**, **spinach**, **carrots**, **peas**, **broccoli**, **eggplant**). Chop up your leftover **chicken or meat loaf**. Stretch the cheese with grated cheese scraps. You can even stretch these leftovers by incorporating them into a béchamel, and use this mixture as one layer along with your pasta, meat or chicken, cheese, and tomato sauce. Let your imagination rule!

BASIC PROCEDURE for LASAGNA
(Serves 4-6)

Following the instructions on the package, boil in salted water to the "al dente" stage

10 to 12 strips **lasagna**

(The number depends on the exact size of your dish and of the strips themselves.) You will need 3 layers.

Drain, rinse briefly under cold water to prevent sticking, and set aside.

Preheat oven to **375°** F.

Grease   **an 8- x 12-inch ovenproof dish**

Either make from scratch

| 4 to 6 c. | **tomato sauce** (see pages 11 and 14) |
| *Or* use | **store-bought pasta sauce** |

Incorporate appropriate   **veggie leftovers**
Set aside.

Chop into small pieces

| about 1 c. | **leftover meat** or **chicken** (**meat loaf** works well) |

Set aside.

If you are not using meat leftovers, sauté about 1 pound of **ground beef** with ¼ cup chopped **onions**, 2 chopped **garlic** cloves, and 1 chopped small **carrot** (to add color and a touch of sweetness). Add 2 Tbs. **red wine** if desired. Set aside.

| Have on hand | 16 oz. | **ricotta cheese** |
| | ¼ c. | **grated Parmesan cheese** |

To ASSEMBLE the LASAGNA

Place 3 or 4 strips of lasagna on bottom of ovenproof dish. Cover with half the meat mixture, then one-third of the tomato sauce. Spread on half the ricotta. Repeat this procedure, ending with 3 to 4 lasagna strips covered with the last third of the tomato sauce. Sprinkle on the Parmesan and dribble 1 Tbs. **olive oil** over the whole.

Place in preheated oven and bake for about **50 minutes**.

POLENTA

Polenta is the Italian name for hominy grits (coarsely ground cornmeal). I have become an enthusiastic fan of polenta as an all-purpose accompaniment to many dishes. It is another true comfort food, especially when combined with a creamed dish. Thus it becomes an elegant backdrop for any number of leftovers. Cooking polenta is as simple as boiling rice. Then all you need to do is to make a béchamel, adding your leftovers. Polenta will firm up beautifully as it cools, and when you invert it, it has a lovely sheen. You can serve it simply side-by-side with slices of meat or chicken, or you can make a ring or mold of the polenta and pour the filling in the center. The polenta should be served hot.

BASIC RECIPE for a POLENTA DISH
(Serves 6)

For the POLENTA

Bring to boil	4 c.	**salted water**
Slowly sprinkle in while stirring		
	1 c.	**grits** (coarsely ground cornmeal)

Be careful of being burned as the mixture comes to a boil because it spurts. Simmer gently for **25 to 30 minutes**, stirring frequently.

Towards the end, add

4 Tbs. (½ stick) **butter**
⅓ c. (or more) **grated cheese**

Moisten the bottom of a **large baking dish** and spread the mixture evenly in it. It will stiffen up as it cools.

When cold, cut into desired shapes, which you can fry as an accompaniment to meat or seafood. Fried polenta is a perfect complement to vegetable dishes.

For the FILLING

Depending on the size of the polenta ring or dish and the quantity of your leftovers, make   1 to 2 c.   **béchamel** (2:2:1; see page 8)

You can make it with milk or any appropriate stock or mixture of the two. If too bland, add   **a bouillon cube**

Stir in chopped leftover vegetables, for example **spinach**, **beans**, **peas**, **carrots**, **corn**, etc. Or you can make a main dish of this with chopped **ham**, **cooked shrimp or chicken**.
Add seasonings according to your leftovers.

Make sure the filling is not stiff, as it will lose moisture during reheating. Add milk or stock if needed.

OTHER WAYS TO SERVE POLENTA

❖ Here is a presentation that always makes a sensation! When the polenta is cooked, allow it to cool slightly and pour it into a greased ring mold. When cold, invert onto an oven-proof platter and fill the center with a creamed filling (see below). Warm the platter in the oven before serving.
❖ Pour a half to three-quarter-inch layer into greased custard cups. When cold, invert. These make attractive rounds to be fried or reheated in the oven.
❖ Pour polenta into a greased bowl and invert when cold. This will give you a mound around which you can arrange the filling.

NOTE: Although coarsely-ground cornmeal makes the best polenta, you can use regular cornmeal. Follow the label for cooking times.

COUSCOUS

Couscous is coarsely ground hard durum wheat, or semolina, of Middle Eastern origin. Its consistency resembles grits or coarsely ground cornmeal. It is easy to prepare and can be a nice change from the usual pastas. All sorts of cut-up leftovers can be mixed into it. Serve it either hot or cold as a salad.

Supermarkets sell "instant" couscous, which usually comes in 10-ounce packages and takes under 10 minutes to prepare. For regular couscous, you will need more liquid and longer cooking time. Whichever you use, follow the instructions on the package.

Packages of "instant" couscous come in many flavor varieties, which you can choose according to your leftovers. Pieces of cooked meat (**beef, lamb, pork**) make good warm main dishes; chopped cooked **vegetables** can be incorporated into plain, cooked couscous for a delicious side dish. Cold cooked **seafood** is especially recommended for use as a salad. **Chicken** is good warm or in a salad.

SIMPLE COUSCOUS SALAD
(Serves 4)

Following the instructions on the package, prepare

10 oz.	**"instant" couscous**

Fluff it gently with a fork and let stand in a bowl until cold.

Meanwhile, chop

½ bunch	**parsley**
2	**scallions**

Stir carefully into the cooled couscous.

Add	1 c.	**cooked seafood**, chopped
	Or 1 c.	**pieces of cooked chicken**
	1 Tbs.	**lemon juice** (only if using plain couscous)

Serve on a lettuce leaf, accompanied by some **cucumber** and **celery** sticks.

VARIATION: Remove the seeds from and make small cubes of a **cucumber**. Salt the cubes and drain for an hour to release their water. Stir into the couscous with the seafood or chicken.

COUSCOUS and MEAT

Since couscous originated in North Africa and is widely used in the Middle East, **lamb** is the obvious meat to reheat with it. But the following recipe works with **pork**, **beef**, and **ham** as well. You can experiment with spices and herbs if you are using plain couscous. **Cumin**, **turmeric**, **cinnamon**, and **nutmeg** are all possibilities. **Mint** is classic with lamb. Here is a sample of what you can do.

(Serves 4)

In a large pan, sauté together

2 Tbs.	**olive oil**
1	**onion** or 3 **scallions**, chopped
1 Tbs.	**garlic**, chopped

When wilted, stir in

1½ to 2 c.	**cooked lamb** cut into ½-inch cubes
1 tsp.	**herbes de Provence** or ground **rosemary**

Cook a few minutes over medium heat till browned.

Moisten with   ¼ to ½ c.   **diced tomatoes**, fresh or canned

Simmer for a few minutes and set aside.

Meanwhile, prepare according to the package directions

     10 oz.   **plain "instant" couscous**

Fluff the couscous with a fork and gently stir in the lamb mixture. Serve this combination warm with **tomato sauce** if desired.

VARIATIONS

- ❖ Leave out the tomatoes and add 2 Tbs. chopped **mint**. Serve with **plain yogurt**.
- ❖ If using beef, pork, or ham, try adding 1 to 2 tsp. **mustard**.
- ❖ With ham or pork, you can add a sweet ingredient, such as a little **pineapple** or **mango** cut into small cubes.
- ❖ **Raisins**, **chopped dates** and **dried apricots**, **pine nuts**, **slivered almonds** are all excellent additions for use with pork, ham, or chicken.
- ❖ Try adding 1 to 2 tsp. **curry** to the meat mix. Leave out the tomatoes.

SUGGESTIONS

Bulghur wheat can replace couscous in the above procedure. See page 129 for bulghur pilaf.

Barley is a great vehicle for using up scraps of lamb. Cook it according to package instructions, using lamb stock if possible. Follow the above procedure and incorporate leftover veggies also, if desired.

CHAPTER 24: RICE

Rice is often left over, as it is difficult to judge quantities required for a dinner gathering. It can be recycled easily by adding a pat of butter, if appropriate, and just warming in the oven or on the stovetop. Don't microwave it, as it will turn into cement. Or it can be added to soups. Rice salad (see page 36) is also delicious. Here I have offered three recipes to help you transform rice leftovers into a new meal.

Following them are three classic recipes to stretch your meat and/or vegetable leftovers. You will cook rice from scratch and use it as a vehicle for carry-overs from yesterday's meal.

RICE SPOON BREAD

This recipe will not only use up leftover **rice**, but also **sour milk** or **cream**. If your milk hasn't turned sour, you can put 1 tsp. of white wine vinegar in 1 cup of milk and let it sit a few minutes. This bread is a good accompaniment to **ham**, or it can be served as a main dish with a **tomato or mushroom sauce** and a **salad**.

(Serves 4)

Preheat oven to **325°** F.

In a small bowl, beat

	2	**eggs**

Melt | 2 Tbs. | **butter** or **shortening** |

Put in a large bowl in this order

1 c.	**boiled rice**
¼ c.	**cornmeal**
2 c.	**sour whole milk** or **half & half**
½ tsp.	**baking soda**
1 tsp.	**salt**

Add the beaten eggs and melted butter. Mix well and pour into a greased 6- x 10-inch oven-proof dish. Bake for **45 minutes** to an hour.

FRIED RICE

Here is a succulent end to that Chinese take-out rice, which has preferably dried out a bit in your fridge. The procedure is super-simple, and the result is as good as the ingredients your imagination has added.

In a skillet, heat	2 Tbs.	**canola or vegetable oil** *Or* use rendered **chicken** **or duck fat** for extra flavor
Add, sauté gently	½	**onion**, chopped
	Or ½ c.	**leeks** (white part), chopped
	Or 2	**scallions**, chopped
	1 Tbs.	**garlic**, chopped
	1 to 2 tsp.	**grated ginger**

When this mixture is translucent, add

	½ tsp.	**sesame seed oil**
	1 to 2 Tbs.	more **fat or oil**
When hot, stir in	1½ to 2 c.	**cooked rice**

If you have some pieces of cooked **chicken**, **meat**, or **seafood** on hand, chop them and add to the mixture.
Cook about **15 minutes** over medium heat while stirring occasionally.

VARIATION: You can moisten the rice with soy sauce or other Asian sauce at the end.

JAMBALAYA

With this traditional Creole dish you can use up cooked rice, meats, and seafood. You start by making a spicy tomato sauce to which you add your meat or seafood ingredients (cooked or raw). Then you stir in the leftover rice and reheat in the oven.

(Serves 4)

In a large skillet, heat		
	2 Tbs.	**oil**
Add	1 medium	**onion**, chopped
	1 stalk	**celery**, chopped
	2 to 3 cloves	**garlic**, coarsely-chopped
	1	**carrot**, peeled and chopped

| | ½ | **bell pepper**, seeded and chopped |

Simmer till softened and barely brown.

Add, simmer 15 to 20 minutes

	1	**14.5-oz. can tomatoes**
	½ c.	**canned tomato sauce**
	2	**bay leaves**
	1 tsp.	**herbes de Provence**, or **thyme**, **basil**, **rosemary**
	1 Tbs.	**Cajun seasoning**
	Or 1 tsp.	**cayenne pepper**
(Optional) Add	½ c.	**ham**, diced
(Optional)	½ c.	**andouille sausage**, diced

Add and simmer **30 minutes**

| | ¼ c. | **white wine** |
| | 1 c. | **chicken stock** (you can use bouillon cube) |

Check seasoning and add salt if necessary, keeping in mind the saltiness of the meat or seafood you will be adding. This is your **basic tomato sauce**, which can be kept a couple of days in the fridge to enhance the flavor.

In a large skillet, sauté gently

| | 2 c. | **cooked or raw chicken** or **seafood**, in pieces |
| | ¼ tsp. | **Cajun seasoning** |

If you are using leftovers, sauté them only a couple of minutes. If using raw ingredients, sauté about **8 minutes**.

Pour on about	1 c.	**reserved tomato sauce**
Add and stir in gently		
	1 c.	**cooked rice**

Correct the seasoning. You may add more meat pieces and sauce for desired consistency. Put in ovenproof dish and heat in **350°** F oven about **20 minutes**.

RISOTTO

Here is a recipe for basic risotto enhanced with cut-up pieces of cooked meat or shrimp and made even better by using appropriately-flavored stock. If you cannot find the requisite **Arborio rice** to make your risotto, you can use the regular short-grained variety (long-grained gets too mushy). The ratio of rice to liquid is much higher than that of regular boiled rice: 1:4. The liquid can be stock or bouillon cubes dissolved in hot water (1 cube to a cup). Nuke it while you are preparing the rest. The whole process will require about **40 minutes** of your full attention.

(Serves about 6)

In large saucepan, heat

	2 Tbs.	**olive oil**

Sauté gently 3 minutes

	½	**onion**, chopped
	½ stalk	**celery**, chopped
	½	**carrot**, chopped
	2 cloves	**garlic**, chopped

Turn up heat to medium.

	Add 1 c.	**Arborio rice**

Stir until rice is no longer translucent and barely beginning to brown, about 2 to 3 minutes.

Stir in until completely absorbed

	¼ to ⅓ c.	**white wine**

Meanwhile, heat in microwave

	3½ to 4 c.	**stock**

Set the timer for **25 minutes**. From now on, you will be adding the hot stock half a cup at a time, stirring gently as you go. After each addition, stir until all the liquid is absorbed before adding more. The rice should be expanding as it absorbs the liquid. Before the last addition, check the seasoning and add some **herbes de Provence** if appropriate.

(Optional) Add	¼ c.	**grated cheese**
Then stir in	½ c.	**leftover meat, chicken, ham,** or **shrimp**

After 25 minutes if the rice seems too dry or is still a bit hard, add some more hot stock and stir 5 minutes more. I like a runny risotto, so I usually add an extra ¼ cup of liquid.

PAELLA

Paella is a Spanish version of a kind of risotto made with seafood and chorizo sausage, seasoned with saffron, which gives it its yellow color. But you can invent your own version, using either leftover rice or leftover hot sausage, chicken, and/or seafood. Since saffron threads are very expensive, you can sacrifice its delicate flavor but retain the yellow color by substituting turmeric.

(Serves 4 to 6)

In a wide, deep frying pan sauté gently together

2 Tbs.	**olive oil**
2 cloves	**garlic**, chopped
1 medium	**onion**, chopped

When wilted, add

1	**14-oz. can tomatoes**

Simmer until beginning to caramelize (10 to 15 minutes).

Stir in   1 c.   **short-grained rice**

Cook until light brown.

Add   2 c.   **boiling water** or **chicken stock**

     1 tsp.   **salt**

Stir and let simmer for 10 minutes.

Add	½ c.	**cooked hot sausage**, cubed
	½ c.	**cooked chicken pieces**
	½ c.	**cooked shrimp**, chopped
(Optional)	½ c.	**cooked mussels** or **clams**
	¼ to ½ tsp.	**turmeric** or **saffron threads**

Continue to simmer for 10 to 15 more minutes. Rice should be cooked through but not mushy. If too dry, add 1 to 2 Tbs. stock. Shake the pan occasionally. For a professional touch, brown the bottom for a minute on high heat. Let stand 5 minutes before serving.

RICE or BULGHUR WHEAT PILAF

With this recipe you can use up leftover cooked rice or leftover veggies and/ or meat. With bulghur, the traditional meat is lamb.

(Serves 4)

With LEFTOVER RICE or BULGHUR

Over low heat, sauté until barely browned (about 10 minutes)

| | 2 Tbs. | **olive oil** |
| | 2 c. | **lamb**, cut into small chunks |

Add and simmer till soft

	1	**carrot**
	1 medium	**onion**, chopped
Add	1 tsp.	**chili pepper**, minced
Moisten with	1 to 2 Tbs.	**stock**

Simmer 2 to 3 minutes and stir in

| | 2 c. | **cooked rice or bulghur** |

Keep over low heat until heated through. Serve hot.

Good with cucumber salad (see page 39) or plain yogurt mixed with chopped mint.

With LEFTOVER MEAT and VEGETABLES

Simmer together the above meat and vegetable ingredients till soft.

| Add | 1 c. | **rice or bulghur** |

Stir until rice or bulghur is golden brown.

| Add and stir | 2 c. | **boiling water** |

Simmer for **20 minutes**. Serve hot.

VARIATION: Add 1 tsp. **curry** to the vegetables for an Indian flavor.

NOTE: See page 36 for **RICE SALAD**.
Also see page 148 for **RICE PUDDING**.

CHAPTER 25:
DUMPLINGS & QUENELLES

DUMPLINGS

Minced, cooked meat, chicken, or fish can be mixed with a flour, egg, and milk batter to make delicious dumplings. Serve them with a sauce and a salad for a light lunch. They are best when made with a highly seasoned leftover mix.

BASIC DUMPLING RECIPE
(Makes about ten 1½-inch dumplings)

In a wide pot, bring to a simmer

about 4 c.	**stock**

Meanwhile, in a large bowl, sift together

1 c.	**flour**
2 tsp.	**baking powder**
½ tsp.	**salt**

Mix together in a small bowl and add to flour mixture

1	**egg**
¼ c.	**milk**

Beat well.

Add and mix in well

1 c.	**cooked meat**, **chicken**, or **fish**, minced

If you have time, chill this dough or let it sit to make it easier to handle. Drop it by spoonfuls into the simmering stock. Do not overcrowd the pan or let the stock come to a hard boil. Cover and simmer gently for about **5 minutes**. Turn the dumplings, cover, and simmer **another 5 minutes**. They should have doubled in size and be light and fluffy. Serve them right away. Save the stock for use in soups, gravies, or béchamels.

NOTE: Depending on the flavor of the dumplings, you could serve them with a **tomato**, **cheese**, or **mushroom** sauce. Fish-based dumplings are good with a lemon-flavored béchamel.

SOUR MILK or HALF & HALF DUMPLINGS

Remember that you can use sour milk or half & half in recipes calling for **buttermilk**. Just add ½ tsp. baking soda per 1 cup flour. The dough for these dumplings can be dropped onto simmering stews or chili for a hearty, complete meal. Or it can be simmered in salted water or stock and served on the side.

Sift into a bowl

¾ c.	**cornmeal**
¼ c.	**flour**
1 tsp.	**baking powder**
¼ tsp.	**baking soda**

In another bowl, mix

¾ c.	**sour milk** or **half & half**
2 Tbs.	**butter**, unsalted, melted
1	**egg**

Combine the two mixtures, beating them briefly. Do not over mix. If mixture seems too liquid, add a little flour. The batter should be slightly stiff.

Drop the batter by small spoonfuls into simmering salted water or broth and simmer, covered, for about **15 minutes**. Do not crowd the dumplings, as they will swell as they cook.

You can use these dumplings in soups, or put a little butter on them and serve as a side dish with meat or chicken.

VARIATION: Drop by spoonfuls fairly far apart onto simmering **stew or chili**. Cover and simmer for about **15 minutes**.

———

QUENELLES

Quenelles are a kind of dumpling made with **cream puff paste**, known in French as *pâte à choux*. This dough should not be confused with **puff pastry** *(pâte feuilletée)*, which is a butter-enriched dough used for pies and croissants. Cream puff paste is a basic procedure used in both salty and sweet recipes. You can use it for dumplings, or you can make puffs that can be stuffed with creamed cooked food. See pages 133 and 134 for further comments about cream puff paste.

For convenience, I am repeating the procedure from Chapter 14, page 77.

BASIC CREAM PUFF PASTE (*PÂTE À CHOUX*)
(Makes about 2 cups)

Have at room temperature

4	**eggs**

In a large saucepan, bring to a boil over medium heat

1 c.	**water**
5 Tbs.	**butter**
pinch	**salt**

When the butter is melted, remove from heat and add all at once

1 c.	**flour**

Beat rapidly with a sturdy wooden spoon, return to heat and continue beating until the mixture thickens and pulls away from the sides of the pan. Remove from heat.

One by one beat in the 4 eggs, making sure each one is absorbed before adding the next. Beat until smooth. You are now ready to use the paste for quenelles or to bake it for puff shells. It will make 16 to 18 shells.

PROCEDURE for MAKING QUENELLES

When you have made the cream puff paste as described above, proceed as follows.

(Makes about twenty 2-inch quenelles)

Add to the above dough

about 1 c. **ground leftover meat, chicken, or fish**

These leftovers need to be as dry as possible, therefore mashing them with a mortar and pestle or a fork might work better than using a blender.

Mix well and let stand in refrigerator an hour or more to stiffen the dough.

When you are ready to cook the quenelles, in a wide sauce pan, bring to simmer   4 to 6 c.   **salted water**

Remove dough from fridge. It should be very stiff. If too stiff to handle, beat in little by little 1 to 3 Tbs.   **heavy whipping cream**

But be careful! Do not let the consistency become soft. It needs to be very firm to keep its shape while poaching.*

Dip two dessert spoons into a bowl of cold water. Fill one spoon with dough. Cup the other over it and use it to help slide the egg-shaped quenelle into the simmering water. Repeat as quickly as possible, but do not crowd the quenelles.

Poach them for about 15 minutes, until they are puffy and roll over easily. You can insert a toothpick into them to check for doneness. Remove with a slotted spoon to drain on a paper towel.

If you are not serving them immediately, brush them with a little melted butter and cover with waxed paper. To reheat, put in a warm oven in a greased oven-proof dish, covered with an appropriate sauce. A mushroom sauce goes well (see page 11). Do not let the sauce overpower the delicate flavor of the quenelles.

* If, as occasionally happens to me, the quenelle paste turns out to be irretrievably too soft, don't despair! You can rename it a mousse and spoon it into a greased pan or ramekins placed in a pan of hot water. Bake at 350°F for about 45 minutes.

When slightly browned on top and beginning to look dry around the edges, remove from water and let set a few minutes. Run a knife around the edge and invert onto serving plate. Garnish with a mushroom or tomato sauce.

PROCEDURE for MAKING *PÂTE À CHOUX* (CREAM PUFF PASTE) SHELLS for STUFFING

In this procedure, you are making *pâte à choux* shells that you will serve warm, stuffed with a creamed filling. You can also serve small ones cold as canapés.

After you have made the basic *pâte à choux* dough (see page 132), drop small mounds of it onto a greased baking sheet. Bake at **400° F** for **10 minutes**. Lower the heat to **350° F** and bake for another **25 minutes**. Make sure the puffs are firm before taking them out of the oven.

To serve warm, cut the tops off and stuff them with any of the following creamed fillings, replacing the tops. The filling should be well seasoned to counteract the blandness of the pastry shell.

Heat for **20 minutes** in a **350° F** oven.

SUGGESTIONS for FILLINGS

- ❖ Curried shrimp or chicken
- ❖ Chopped chicken, shrimp in thick béchamel (for croquettes, see page 75)
- ❖ Chopped ham in cheese sauce
- ❖ Spinach, mushrooms, and onions in thick béchamel. Make the spinach as dry as possible when adding to the béchamel.
- ❖ See "Suggestions for Stuffed Crêpes" on page 63.

FISH or SEAFOOD QUENELLES

This is an elegant way to use up that odd filet of fish or some leftover shrimp. The trick is to have all the ingredients very cold so that the quenelles will hold together when you form them. You will be using a *pâte à choux* base into which you will incorporate a purée of fish or seafood. The traditional quenelle recipe calls for uncooked fish, but it is perfectly acceptable to use fish in its cooked state. Here is a starter recipe for quenelles made with a leftover filet of flounder and some crabmeat.

(Serves 5 to 6, makes about 30 quenelles)

Make the basic **Pâte à choux** (see page 77)

Pulse in a blender

2 c. **cooked fish, shrimp, crabmeat,** or other **seafood**

Try to keep this purée as dry as possible. If it is too difficult to mix in the blender, mash it with a fork. Beat it vigorously into the *pâte à choux*. The mixture should be very stiff.

Add and beat   a pinch   **grated nutmeg**
                      a pinch   **white pepper**

Place the pan as is in the fridge till the mixture is thoroughly chilled.

When you are ready to poach the quenelles, bring a large pan of lightly salted water to the simmer. If you have fish stock, all the better.

Have a small bowl with ice water handy. Shape the quenelles by dipping a soup or dessert spoon into the ice water and scooping out some batter with it. In your other hand take another same-sized spoon and smooth the top with it. Loosen the dough by sliding the second spoon under the dough and dropping the quenelles into the gently simmering water. Simmer very gently uncovered for **15 to 20 minutes**. Be careful not to crowd them, as they will swell up.

Remove to a warm dish. Serve with a cream and mushroom sauce, as suggested below.

———————————

CREAM and MUSHROOM SAUCE for QUENELLES
(Makes 1½ cups)

In a sauce pan, simmer together

2 Tbs.	**butter** or **margarine**
1 c.	**mushrooms**, sliced
¼ c.	**onions**, chopped
Or ¼ c.	*mirepoix* mix (see page 12)

When all the moisture is evaporated and the mushrooms slightly browned, sprinkle with

2 Tbs.	**flour**

Add and stir

½ c.	**stock**
½ c.	**half & half** or **whipping cream**
¼ c.	**white wine**

Bring to a simmer and cook for about **10 minutes**. Correct the seasoning, but don't overdo it. You don't want to overshadow the delicate taste of the quenelles.

———————

CHAPTER 26: BREAD

I have always felt that bread was sacred, so all my life I tried to save the scraps. When they get to be overwhelming, I deal with them in a couple of simple ways, by either cutting them into cubes for croutons or making bread crumbs. To save stale bread, it's best just to let it dry out in an unsealed container, like a paper bag, at room temperature.

The following procedures are for both transforming stale bread and for making new bread from leftover ingredients, such as sour milk or cream.

WORKING with STALE BREAD

BREAD CRUMBS

What an easy way to save money at the supermarket! Just grind your **dried bread scraps** in a food processor (better) or a blender. You can add dried herbs if you like, but I prefer to keep the flavor neutral for use in both sweet and salty dishes. Grind to your preferred coarseness and put in a sealed jar. For guaranteed freshness, keep in refrigerator.

If you don't have a blender, place broken-up dried bread pieces in a sealed plastic bag and bang them with a roller. Then roll them until the desired texture is obtained.

Stale **potato** or **corn chips** make good crumbs. If they're soggy, crisp them up in a warm oven. Make sure they are not rancid.

Sometimes recipes call for **"soft bread crumbs"**. For these you need not-too-stale bread (2 to 4 days old). Pull the pieces apart with a fork in order not to mash them. When measuring, spoon them lightly into the measuring cup. If not using right away, store them in a tightly-sealed container in the fridge for up to a few days. They will start to mold after that.

CROUTONS

Cut **dried bread slices** into cubes, if possible. Even broken pieces are OK. Sauté gently in **cooking oil**. (I like a combination of canola and olive oil.) Be careful that they don't burn. Add a little **salt** and **pepper** and some **dried**

herbs (optional) and put in a sealed jar, which should be kept in the fridge to prevent them from becoming rancid.

Another way is to place bread cubes on a baking sheet and put in a **300°** F oven **20 to 30 minutes** until they are completely dry and crisp. These croutons are taste-neutral and can be used in sweet puddings.

FRIED BREAD

If you're not too worried about your cholesterol level, fried bread slices will add a delicious touch to open-faced sandwiches; or scrambled, fried, or poached eggs; or creamed dishes. Sautéed stale bread slices in bacon fat or olive oil are especially tasty.

For a quick breakfast or lunch, fry some **bacon** slices and remove to drain on a paper towel. In the hot fat, sauté stale **bread slices**; remove to plate. Then sauté some **onion** and **tomato** (green or red) slices, adding a little oil if the fat gives out. Remove to a plate and make the **eggs** as you please. Serve over the fried bread accompanied by the bacon strips.

Pieces of fried bread are also a hearty addition to a mixed salad.

FRENCH TOAST

This is an old standby. You can also use up slightly sour milk.

(Serves 4)

In a shallow dish, mix together

2	**eggs**
about ½ c.	**milk** or **half & half**

Dip into the mixture

4 slices	**stale bread**

Leave until the bread becomes thoroughly saturated. This might take 15 or 20 minutes.

Sauté the slices on both sides in **butter**, **margarine**, or **oil** over medium heat until a crisp crust forms, and serve with **syrup** or **jam**. Or sprinkle with **cinnamon** and/or **sugar**. What a great breakfast!

CROUTON STUFFING for a TURKEY or a LARGE CHICKEN

This is an all-purpose poultry stuffing that has proven its worth over the years. It is endlessly adaptable. My preference is for sautéed croutons (see above), as they have built-in flavor.

In a large skillet over medium heat, melt

	2 to 3 Tbs.	**vegetable oil**
Add and sauté until wilted		
	1 medium	**onion**, chopped
	1 stalk	**celery**, chopped
	1	**carrot**, finely chopped
	2 cloves	**garlic**, chopped
(Optional)	½ c.	**mushrooms**, sliced
(Optional)	the chopped	**liver** and **heart** from the bird
Add	3 to 4 c.	**croutons**

When lightly browned, add

	¼ c.	**parsley**, chopped
		zest of 1 lemon
	1 Tbs.	**herbes de Provence**
		Or **herbs** of your choice (**sage** is superb)
Season with		**salt** and **pepper**
Stir in	¼ c.	**white wine**
(Optional)	1 Tbs.	**whiskey** (a nice addition!)
	¼ c.	**chicken stock**

Add a little more chicken stock if stuffing seems too dry, but be careful not to let it get soggy. Spoon stuffing lightly into bird's neck and breast cavities. Fasten with toothpicks or sew shut.

SUGGESTION

If your crowd doesn't like **chicken livers**, chop and sauté them separately anyway, but put them aside. Then when you make the gravy, add them and let them simmer a while. At serving time, strain the gravy. The livers will have added depth to the flavor. Save them for recycling in, say, **rice** or **couscous**, or for a **canapé** (see pages 21 and 22).

CHEESE MELT or *"CROÛTE AU FROMAGE"*

I'm not sure if "melt" is the right name for *"croûte au fromage"*, which is a classic open-faced grilled cheese sandwich popular in Switzerland, France, and Belgium. It is so simple and so good! If you have some real Swiss (Gruyère) cheese, all the better, but otherwise sharp or extra-sharp cheddar or Monterey Jack will do. You can use up scraps of other hard cheeses, too. Supermarket Swiss is OK, but you should jazz up its blandness with some other sharp cheese.

(Serves 4)

Toast   4 slices   **stale bread**

(Optional) Pour into an oven-proof dish
                   ¼ c.   **white wine**

Place toast in the ovenproof dish and top with
                   2 c.   **grated cheese**

Put under medium broiler till cheese is melted and lightly browned. Serve with mustard, sour pickles, or onions.

VARIATIONS: You can vary this procedure by putting **sliced tomatoes** under the cheese, and/or **bacon** on top of it. Another popular variation is a poached or fried **egg** on top (which you have cooked separately).

NOTE: You can stretch the grated cheese by mashing it with a splash of half & half.

———————————

MAKING BREADS USING SOUR MILK or CREAM

With the price of milk these days, it can be distressing to find your milk or half & half turning sour. Don't despair. Try one of these easy recipes to make breads that will be crowd pleasers and family tummy-fillers.

HOW TO MAKE SOUR MILK

If you have the urge to make a recipe with sour milk or one that calls for **buttermilk** and yours is still fresh, just add 1 tsp. **white vinegar** or **lemon juice** to 1 cup **milk** and let stand for 10 minutes.

———————————

SOUR MILK CORN BREAD

This recipe makes a finely textured bread.

(Serves 6)

Preheat oven to **425°** F.

Sift together	1 c.	**flour**
	½ tsp.	**baking soda**
	2 tsp.	**baking powder**
	1 to 2 Tbs.	**sugar**
	1½ tsp.	**salt**
Stir in	¾ c.	**yellow cornmeal**

In another bowl beat together

	1 c.	**sour milk**
	2	**eggs**
	3 Tbs.	**melted butter** or **bacon fat**

Combine all ingredients. Pour into a 6- x 10-inch ovenproof dish and bake for **30 minutes**.

SOUR MILK BISCUITS

Biscuits are an all-time favorite and are so easy to make. Using sour milk makes tender dough.

Best results are achieved by pulsing with a food processor. If you don't have one, put ingredients in a large bowl and cut in the butter with a pastry cutter or knife. Butter and milk should be very cold. Handle dough as little as possible to prevent it from becoming tough.

(Makes about 15 two-inch biscuits)

Preheat oven to **425°** F.

Sift together into processor bowl

	2 c.	**flour**
	1 Tbs.	**baking powder**
	¼ tsp.	**baking soda**
	½ tsp.	**salt**

Cut into small pieces and add

5 Tbs. very cold **butter** or **shortening**

Pulse about 6 to 8 times till butter pieces are the size of small peas.

Add   ½ c. very cold **sour milk** or **half & half**

Pulse about 10 times till dough just forms a ball around the blade. If too dry, add a little more sour milk. Do not over-mix!

Turn dough out on a lightly floured surface and pat gently until it is ¾ to 1 inch thick. Cut 2 inch rounds with a cookie cutter or a drinking glass dipped in flour. Place at least one inch apart on and ungreased baking sheet. Bake for **12 to 15 minutes**, depending on thickness and size. Don't let them get brown, only golden.

NOTE: If you plan to use the biscuits with shortcake, add 1 Tbs. **sugar** to the sifted ingredients.

SPOON BREAD

This recipe makes a kind of bread and uses up **sour milk** or **cream**. It's a sort of corn bread, but calls for white cornmeal. Note that you can use your turned milk or cream in many recipes calling for buttermilk.

(Serves 2 to 3)

Preheat oven to **350° F.**
Grease   **a 7-inch pie plate**

Beat together till smooth
                1½ c.   **boiling water**
                1 c.   **white cornmeal**
Allow to cool to lukewarm.

Add and beat   1   **egg**
                1 Tbs.   **melted butter**
                1 c.   **sour milk**
                1 tsp.   **baking soda**
                ¾ tsp.   **salt**

Pour mixture into baking pan and bake for **30 to 40 minutes**. Serve with toppings of butter, jam, honey, maple or other fruit syrup.

SOUR MILK or CREAM SCONES

Scones are basically biscuits enriched by egg and cream. You can experiment with various flavors. My favorite is slightly sweet and uses grated orange rind. The idea comes from Julia Child via a friend.

(Makes about 12 two-inch scones)

Preheat oven to **425°** F.

Have ready | **an ungreased baking sheet**

Sift together into processor bowl

2 c.	**flour**
2 tsp.	**baking powder**
½ tsp.	**baking soda**
½ tsp.	**salt**
3 Tbs.	**sugar**

Add | **zest of 1 large orange**

Cut into small pieces and add

1 stick (4 oz.) **butter**, unsalted, very cold

Pulse briefly until dough looks like fine gravel.

Beat together in small bowl

⅓ c.	**sour milk** or **half & half**
1	**egg**

Add to flour/butter mixture.

Pulse about 10 times until dough just begins to form a ball around the blade. If the dough is too flaky or dry, add a Tbs. of sour milk.

Add	2 Tbs.	**currants** or **raisins**
	2 Tbs.	**dates**, chopped

Pulse about 3 times, just enough to mix the fruit into the dough.

Turn dough out onto a lightly floured surface and pat quickly with finger tips (don't use palms, as they give off too much heat) until it is ¾ to 1 inch thick. Cut 2 inch rounds with a cookie cutter or a drinking glass dipped in flour. Place at least one inch apart on the ungreased baking sheet. Bake for **12 to 15 minutes**, depending on thickness and size. Don't let them get brown, only golden.

VARIATIONS: You can use grated lemon rind instead of orange. Or omit the zest and add 2 tsp. cinnamon and increase the dates. Candied fruit is also a possibility.

REMINDER: You don't *have* to use a food processor to make biscuits or scones. Cut the butter into the dry ingredients with a pastry cutter or two knives and stir in the liquid ingredients very briefly. Lastly, fold in the dried fruit.

———————

OATMEAL BLUEBERRY MUFFINS

A popular way to use up **sour milk** is to make muffins with it. There are many recipes for muffins made with buttermilk, so just make them with your turned milk. Here is a tasty and hearty version. It is not too sweet. The only hitch is that you have to remember to soak the oats ahead of time.

(Makes 12 muffins)

Preheat oven to **375°** F.

Grease **muffin pans** or line them with papers.

In a large bowl, soak together for at least an hour, preferably overnight

1 c.	**oats**, any kind
1 c.	**sour milk**

Sift together and put aside

1 c.	**flour**
2½ tsp.	**baking powder**
½ tsp.	**baking soda**
1 tsp.	**cinnamon**
¼ tsp.	**salt**

In a small bowl, whisk together

2	**eggs**
½ c.	**brown sugar**
¼ c.	**canola oil** (or other vegetable oil)

Stir this mixture into the oat mixture.

Fold in the sifted dry ingredients until just mixed. Do not overbeat or worry about a few lumps.

Fold in	½ to ¾ c.	**blueberries**, fresh or thawed and drained

Pour into prepared pans and bake for **20 to 25 minutes**. The muffins should be light brown and spring back to the touch. You can give them the toothpick test just to be sure.

VARIATION: You can leave out the **blueberries** for a tasty plain variety.

For a recipe for BANANA BREAD, see CHAPTER 30: FRUITS, page 172.

For recipes using stale bread in desserts, see CHAPTER 27: SWEET PUDDINGS, pages 146 and 147, and CHAPTER 28: CREAM DESSERTS, pages 149 to 151.

CHAPTER 27: SWEET PUDDINGS

Puddings are usually sweet, but the procedure can also be used for vegetables, as we have seen in Chapter 20. They are a kind of hearty custard, using a mix of eggs and milk or cream to bind various ingredients. Bread or rice puddings spring to mind, both of which I would classify as thoroughly comfort food and an economical way to feed a hungry family. The recipes for bread pudding are ideal ways to use up stale bread.

BREAD and BUTTER PUDDING
(Serves 4 to 6)

Preheat oven to **350°** F.

Butter, leaving crusts on

	8 slices	**stale white bread**

Place 4 slices, butter side up, on bottom of a buttered baking dish.

Sprinkle with	1 Tbs.	**candied fruit***
	2 Tbs.	**currants** or **raisins**

Cover with second layer of 4 buttered bread slices.

Sprinkle with	2 more Tbs.	**currants** or **raisins**

In a bowl, beat	3	**eggs**
Add	1¼ c.	**milk**
	⅓ c.	**heavy cream** (or use more **half & half**, less milk)
Beat in	¼ c.	**sugar**
	about 1 tsp.	**lemon zest**

Pour mixture over the bread.

Dust with		**grated nutmeg**

Bake in oven for **30 to 40 minutes**. Serve warm. Maple syrup goes well with it.

* For added flavor, you can soak the candied fruit in rum or other liqueur beforehand.

OLD-FASHIONED BREAD PUDDING

The nice thing about this recipe is that you can use stale **whole wheat bread** as well as white. Leave crusts on. You can also use stale **croissants**. This is a delightful and elegant recipe, worthy of company when served with a vanilla sauce (*crème anglaise*, see page 149).

(Serves 6)

Preheat oven to **350° F.**

Butter   **a 6- x 10-inch ovenproof dish**

Break into pieces

	2 c.	**stale bread slices**
Soak them in	2 c.	**milk**

Let soak for about half an hour. Mix well to remove lumps. If still too lumpy, pulse in blender.

Add and mix well

3 oz. (¾ stick)	**melted butter**
½ c.	**brown sugar** (or granulated)
2	**eggs**, beaten
2 tsp.	**mixed spices** (e.g. nutmeg, cinnamon, ginger)
1 c.	**dried fruit** (raisins, figs, dates, currants, candied peel, etc.), chopped
	zest of 1 orange

Pour mixture into the buttered baking dish. Sprinkle with grated nutmeg or cookie or cake crumbs (optional). Bake for about **1 hour**. The pudding should be brown and bubbly. It can be served warm or cold. Try it with a custard sauce (*crème anglaise*, page 149) or vanilla ice cream.

NOTE: If you like candied fruit, you can add it and enhance the pudding's flavor by soaking it in rum for a couple of hours beforehand.

RICE PUDDING

This is a great way to use up that steamed rice you brought home in a doggie bag.

(Serves about 6)

Preheat oven to **325° F.**

Butter **a 6- x 10-inch ovenproof dish**

In a bowl, beat together

1½ c.	**milk**
pinch	**salt**
4 Tbs.	**sugar** or ½ c. **brown sugar**
1 Tbs.	**butter**, melted or soft
1 tsp.	**vanilla**
3	**eggs**

Add and mix gently

1½ c.	**cooked rice**
	zest of 1 lemon or **orange**
1 tsp.	**lemon juice**
½ c.	**dried fruit, chopped** (golden raisins are nice)

Pour the rice mixture into a buttered baking dish. Sprinkle lightly with cookie or bread crumbs. Bake for about **50 minutes**. Serve with a fruit *coulis* (see page 168) or vanilla ice cream.

CHAPTER 28: CREAM DESSERTS

You can make interesting desserts of stale **cake** or leftover **sweetened bread**, like cinnamon bread, breakfast bread, raisin bread, stollen, etc., by combining them with a **custard cream**, **whipped cream**, and/or **meringue**. You can use your imagination to combine these ingredients. The result is rather like a stiff trifle or a tiramisu. It should be made several days ahead, as the flavor builds as it sits in your fridge.

The basic procedure is to make a garden-variety vanilla cream or pudding, which you will spread over the stale bread that has been soaked in some kind of liqueur. There are two kinds of vanilla cream/pudding, known either as *"crème anglaise"* or *"crème pâtissière,"* which use the same ingredients. The former, made with only egg yolks, sugar, and milk that by no means must come to the boil, is more fluid; the latter is stiffer, as you will cook it with some added flour. They are both quite simple to make.

You can spread your creation with one of three suggested kinds of toppings, or you can leave it as is.

BASIC PROCEDURE for a CREAM DESSERT

CRÈME ANGLAISE
(Makes about 2 cups)

Put in a heavy-bottomed saucepan or the top of a double boiler, and bring to a simmer over medium heat (to prevent scorching)

1¾ c.	**milk**

(If you would like a chocolate or coffee flavor, dissolve 2 to 3 oz. **semi-sweet chocolate** or 1 Tbs. **instant coffee** in the boiling milk.)

Meanwhile, in a medium bowl, beat

	4	**egg yolks**
Add	½ c.	**sugar**
	1½ tsp.	**cornstarch**

If your milk has turned a little sour, add

	½ tsp.	**baking soda**

Beat well, about **2 minutes**, till the mixture falls from the whisk or beaters in wide ribbons. Stir in the simmering milk. Return the mixture to the saucepan or top of double boiler.

If using just a sauce pan, place over low heat. Stir *gently* but constantly while heating the mixture to **170°** F, scraping the bottom and not allowing the cream to come to the boil (it will curdle if you do). Stir slowly with a wire whisk to keep it as smooth as possible as it thickens. If you beat it too vigorously, the *crème* will foam, and it will be difficult to watch the thickening process.

If using a double boiler (a safer method), cook mixture in top over, not touching, boiling water. This takes longer, but there is less risk of over-cooking the cream.

When the cream reaches the right consistency (it will firm up a bit more when cooled), remove from heat and stir in

1 to 2 tsp.	**vanilla or almond extract, rum, cognac**, or other **liqueur**

Stir occasionally as the cream cools. Put the egg whites aside for possible use as a meringue topping (see below, page 151) or in a soufflé (see page 54).

CRÈME PÂTISSIÈRE

(Makes about 2½ cups)

Put in saucepan and bring to simmer

	2 c.	**milk**

Meanwhile, in a large bowl, beat

	5	**egg yolks**
Add	1 c.	**sugar**

Beat well, about 2 minutes till the mixture falls from the whisk or beaters in wide ribbons.

Beat in well	⅔ c.	**flour**

Beat in the simmering milk. Return the mixture to the saucepan, and over medium heat bring to a simmer while beating gently. Make sure to keep scraping the bottom. Boil gently for **2 to 3 minutes** to cook the flour. Remove from heat.

Beat in	1 Tbs.	**butter**
	1½ Tbs.	**vanilla**

(See the *crème anglaise* recipe above for flavor variations.)

Beat occasionally as the cream cools. Save the egg whites for possible use as a meringue topping, for a frosting with egg whites (see below), or for plain meringues. Remember, you can also keep them for a soufflé.

To ASSEMBLE a CREAM DESSERT
(Serves about 8)

Line the bottom of a **7- x 9-inch glass dish** with slices of
stale sweetened bread

Sprinkle with   ¼ c.   **rum** or **liqueur**

If the bread is very hard, add some water to the rum. Let it soak while you make the cream and topping.

(Optional) Sprinkle with some   **candied fruit**

Make the *crème anglaise* recipe above or half the one for *crème pâtissière*. Spread it over the bread slices. Allow it to cool completely before adding one of the following toppings.

TOPPINGS

OPTION 1: MERINGUE TOPPING
(Makes enough to spread on a 7- x 9-inch dish)

Beat until foamy
                    3 to 4   **egg whites**
Gradually beat in
                    10 Tbs. (5 oz.) **sugar**
                    1 tsp.   **vanilla**
(Optional)   1 tsp.   **cream of tartar**

Spread it over the cooled vanilla cream. Place on low shelf in oven under a medium broiler for **5 to 8 minutes** to brown. Keep a watchful eye on it, as meringue burns easily. When cool, cover with plastic wrap and refrigerate at least 24 hours.

See below (page 153) for recipe for **PLAIN MERINGUES**

OPTION 2: WHIPPED CREAM

(Makes enough to spread on a 7- x 9-inch dish)

Whip until stiff	1 c.	**heavy cream**
	2 Tbs.	**sugar**
	½ tsp.	**vanilla**

Spread over the cooled vanilla cream. Sprinkle on some **cookie crumbs** or shake a little **cocoa** powder over the top. Cover with plastic wrap and refrigerate at least 24 hours.

OPTION 3: FROSTING with EGG WHITES

(Makes enough to spread on a 7- x 9-inch dish)

Mix in top of double boiler		
2	**egg whites**, unbeaten
½ c.	**sugar**
5 Tbs.	**water**
pinch	**salt**
½ tsp.	**cream of tartar**

Beat with electric mixer over boiling water till stiff (**6 to 10 minutes**).

| Add | 1 to 2 tsp. | **vanilla** or **rum** |

Beat until thick enough to spread.

PLAIN MERINGUES

This is a great way to use up **egg whites**. The trick is to beat them very stiff and dry and bake them in a very slow oven, so that they dry out. After you have baked them, you need to keep them in as dry an environment as possible; otherwise they will lose their crispness and get chewy.

Preheat oven to **225°** F.
Spread parchment or waxed paper on a **baking sheet**.

Beat until foamy		
	3 to 4	**egg whites**
Gradually beat in		
	10 Tbs. (5 oz.)	**sugar**
	1 tsp.	**vanilla**
(Optional)	1tsp.	**cream of tartar**

Continue beating until very stiff and dry.

Spoon meringue mixture in mounds onto the baking sheet and bake for **1 to 2 hours**, depending on size. Turn off heat, leave door closed, and let cool and dry out in the oven.

Remove to a tin and keep tightly sealed to maintain crispness.

NOTE: If you want to stuff the meringues with, say, **ice cream** or a **vanilla cream filling** (*crème pâtissière*, page 150), remove them while still warm and poke the flat side with your thumb, but put them back in the oven till they're completely cold. The point is to keep them as dry as possible.

CHAPTER 29: CAKES

Sour milk or cream can be put to good use with spice cakes. The following recipe has been unabashedly borrowed from *The Joy of Cooking*. Since Irma Rombauer was my kitchen mentor for many long years, her methods have seeped into my repertoire. It is a good idea to remove the butter, eggs, and sour milk from the fridge ahead of time so that they come to room temperature. If by any chance you don't have sour milk and have forgotten to leave it out on the counter overnight, you can create it by adding ½ tsp. lemon juice or white wine vinegar to your regular milk and letting it stand a few minutes.

SPICE CAKE (Inspired by *Joy of Cooking*)

This cake is nice and light and doesn't have an overpowering spicy flavor. The orange glaze makes it more interesting.

Preheat oven to **350°** F.
Grease   **a 9-inch tube pan**

Have ready   ⅞ c.   **sour milk** (1 c. minus 2 Tbs.)

In a large bowl, cream together
               6 oz. (1½ sticks) **butter**, softened
               1½ c.   **sugar**
Add the sugar gradually and beat until very light and fluffy.

Separate   3   **eggs**
Add the yolks one by one to the butter mixture. Beat in until smooth.

In another bowl, sift together
               1¾ c.   **all-purpose flour**
               Or 2 c.   **cake flour**
               1 tsp.   **baking powder**
               ½ tsp.   **baking soda**
               1 tsp.   **grated nutmeg**
               1 tsp.   **cinnamon**
               ½ tsp.   **ground cloves**
               ½ tsp.   **salt**

Add flour to the butter and egg mixture alternately with the sour milk three times, beating well each time until the batter is smooth.

Beat till firm **the 3 egg whites**

Fold them gently into the batter. Pour into the greased tube pan and bake for **50 to 60 minutes**.

Remove from oven when an inserted toothpick comes out clean. Poke a few small holes with a skewer. Spread the hot cake with orange glaze (see below), allowing it to soak into the cake. As it cools, it will form a light orangey crust. When cake is cool, remove from pan.

ORANGE GLAZE
(Makes enough for a 9-inch tube cake or 2 loaf cakes.)

Beat together	2 Tbs.	**butter**, softened
	⅓ c.	**sugar**
	1 Tbs.	**orange juice**

Spread on a warm cake while it is still in the pan. Remove cake from pan when cool.

BAKED ALASKA

This is a fun dessert and not that difficult to make. The trick is to have the ice cream super hard, like a brick. You can use up **leftover sponge cake** and **egg whites** in one fell swoop. Of course, you must serve the dessert as soon as it comes out of the oven.

STEP 1:
Make a **meringue topping**, using method on page 151, as repeated here.

Beat until foamy

	3 or 4	**egg whites**
Gradually beat in		
	10 Tbs. (5 oz.)	**sugar**
	1 tsp.	**vanilla**
(Optional)	1 tsp.	**cream of tartar**

Continue beating till stiff, but don't overbeat to the point of dryness. Put aside.

STEP 2:

Preheat oven broiler to **highest heat**.

Butter lightly	**a rectangular oven-proof dish**

Line the bottom with	**thick slices of stale sponge cake**
Sprinkle with	**rum** or other **liqueur**

From now on you will need to act very swiftly!

Lay on at least a 1-inch thick slab of **very hard ice cream**.

Cover completely with a layer of **meringue topping**.

Place in middle of oven briefly until the meringue becomes golden brown. Be careful, as meringue burns easily.

Remove from oven quickly and serve immediately.

BANANA CAKE

With this recipe you will use up **over-ripe bananas** as well as **sour milk**. A plain vanilla frosting goes well with it (see below).

Preheat oven to **350° F.**

Grease	**2 round layer pans or a 9- x 13-inch baking pan**

Sift together and put aside

2 c.	**flour**
1 ⅔ c.	**sugar**
1 ¼ tsp.	**baking powder**
1 ¼ tsp.	**baking soda**
1 tsp.	**salt**

Blend together in large bowl

⅔ c. (1 stick plus 2½ Tbs.)	**butter**, softened
⅔ c.	**sour milk**
3	**eggs**

Add alternately with the flour mixture

	1¼ c.	**bananas** (2 to 3 bananas), mashed

Add and mix well

	⅔ c.	**nuts**, finely chopped

Beat the mixture well and pour into greased cake pan(s). Bake the round pans about **35 minutes**, the single pan about **45 minutes**.

Check by inserting a toothpick to see if it comes out clean. Cool for a few minutes before turning out onto a rack.

Use one of the following frostings.

UNCOOKED VANILLA BUTTER FROSTING

Beat together	3 c.	**confectioners' sugar**
	5 Tbs.	**butter**, softened
	Add	1½ tsp. **vanilla**
If too stiff, add	1 to 2 Tbs.	**half & half**

Beat hard until smooth enough to spread.

CREAM CHEESE VANILLA FROSTING

Beat together	3 oz.	**cream cheese**, softened
	1 tsp.	**vanilla**
	1 Tbs.	**milk**
	pinch	**salt**
Add gradually while beating		
	2½ c.	**confectioners' sugar**

Beat vigorously until smooth enough to spread. If too stiff, add a little **milk**.

ORANGE CAKE (From *Betty Crocker's Cookbook*)

Here is an old recipe for a delicately flavored cake to help you use up **sour milk**. The golden raisins give it a special flair.

Preheat oven to **350° F.**
Grease and flour   **two 9-inch round cake pans**

Sift together and put aside

2½ c.	**flour**
1½ c.	**sugar**
1½ c.	**baking soda**
¾ tsp.	**salt**

Beat together in large bowl

	¾ c.	**butter**, softened
	3	**eggs**
Mix in	1½ c.	**sour milk**
	1½ tsp.	**vanilla**
Add	1 c.	**golden raisins**, chopped
	½ c.	**nuts**, finely chopped
	1 Tbs.	**grated orange peel**

Mix until well blended and pour into prepared pans. Bake about **35 minutes**.

When cool, frost with the **uncooked vanilla butter frosting** above, substituting 4 Tbs. **orange juice** for the vanilla and half & half and adding 2 tsp. grated **orange peel**.

———————————

TIRAMISU

Save your stale **coffee** in a glass jar in the fridge until you have a chance to make this fabulous dessert. You will need to buy a 7-oz. package of **ladyfingers** (the hard kind, not the sponge cake kind), which you can probably find in the ethnic foods aisle of your supermarket if you can't in the cookie aisle. The required **Mascarpone** cheese comes in a small container like cottage cheese and is usually found in the special cheeses section.

(Serves 8 to 10)

From your arsenal   **3 bowls**: 2 medium and 1 large
A shallow bowl or dish, for dipping
the ladyfingers
A 6- x 10-inch serving dish
(not metal)

In a medium bowl, combine and beat for 3 minutes

3	**egg yolks**
⅓ c.	**sugar**

In the large bowl, combine and beat until creamy

	8 oz.	**Mascarpone** (Italian cream cheese)*****
(Optional)	1 tsp.	**vanilla**

Add the yolk mixture and beat for another 3 minutes.

In the second medium bowl, beat until very stiff and dry

3	**egg whites**
pinch	**salt**

Gently fold the beaten egg whites into the egg yolk and Mascarpone mixture.

In the same bowl you have used for the egg whites, beat until stiff and put aside   8 oz.   **whipping cream**

* If Mascarpone cheese is not available, combine 4 oz. **cream cheese**, ¼ c. **whipping cream**, and 3 Tbs. **sour cream**.

To ASSEMBLE

Grate coarsely onto a plate

2 oz.	**dark chocolate** (You can use Baker's unsweetened.)

Pour into a shallow dish

about ¾ c.	**strong**, **cold coffee** (the stronger the better)
(Optional)	2 to 3 Tbs.	**Kahlúa** (Mexican coffee liqueur)

Dip the **ladyfingers**, one by one, quickly into the coffee, sugared side up, and lay side by side in serving dish. The trick is not to dip so long that they become soggy. You should use half the ladyfingers (18 if using the Gilda brand) for the bottom layer. You may have to break them to fit empty spaces.

Spread with half the yolk and Mascarpone mixture.

Spread with half the whipped cream.

Repeat the above operation, finishing up all the ingredients.

Sprinkle the grated chocolate over the top layer of whipped cream. Cover with plastic wrap and refrigerate, overnight if possible.

———————

CHAPTER 30: FRUIT

CRUMBLES or CRISPS

Everybody loves fruit crumbles, a. k. a. crisps or crunches. They are a good way to use up odds and ends of fruit that might be going to waste. You can rescue them with the following simple cooking procedure. Recipes for crumbles or crisps use the same ingredients, but the quantities vary widely. You can adapt the proportions according to your arsenal, your sweet tooth, or the fruit you are using. For example, you may not have oats on hand, so just use more flour. Or if you don't have light brown sugar, use the equivalent amount of dark brown or granulated.

You can mix the ingredients by pulsing them in a food processor. But it is really quicker and simpler to rub them together briskly with your fingers in a bowl. However, they should stay as cold as possible so that they don't get gooey. This dessert is good served lukewarm with a scoop of vanilla ice cream.

BASIC CRUMBLE RECIPE

(Serves 5 to 6)

For the TOPPING

Mix together till crumbly

	1 c.	**flour**
	½ c.	rolled **oats** (or quick-cooking)
	½ c.	light **brown sugar** (or mix of dark brown and granulated)
	pinch	**salt** (if butter is unsalted)
(Optional)	½ tsp.	**baking powder**
(Optional)	1 tsp.	**cinnamon** (if using with apples, pears, plums, or rhubarb)
	4 oz.	**unsalted butter**, very cold or frozen, cut in pieces
(Optional)	⅓ c.	**walnuts** or **pecans** chopped

These ingredients can be pulsed for about **20 seconds** in a food processor until they just begin to make small clumps.

You can refrigerate or freeze this topping until you are ready with your fruit mixture. You don't need to defrost it before baking.

For the FRUIT FILLING

Preheat oven to **350° F.**

Butter		**a 6- x 10-inch glass ovenproof dish**

Cut into pieces or slice

	3 to 4 c.	**fruit** (apples, pears, plums, berries)
Add and mix	½ to 1 c.	**sugar**, depending on the acidity of the fruit
	1 to 2 Tbs.	**flour** (higher amount for rhubarb) **zest of 1 lemon**
	1 Tbs.	**lemon juice** or **white wine**
(Optional)	2 tsp.	**cinnamon**

Let this mixture sit a while. Spread it in the buttered Pyrex dish and crumble the topping over it. Place on oven rack in upper part of oven and bake for about **45 minutes**. Serve lukewarm or cold with a scoop of **vanilla ice cream**.

CHERRY CRISP

Sometimes you just can't eat your way through that bowl of cherries before they start getting spots on them. So, you cut them up into pieces and make a crisp. It won't be quite as flavorful as if you had made it with sour cherries, but it will be sweet and good nonetheless. Watch it disappear!

(Serves 4)

Preheat oven to **375° F.**

Butter		**a Pyrex ovenproof dish**

For the FRUIT

Put in bowl	1 to 2 c.	**cherries**, cut into chunks
Add	2 to 3 Tbs.	**sugar**
		zest of 1 lemon
	2 tsp.	**lemon juice**
(Optional)	1 to 2 Tbs.	**kirsch** (cherry brandy) or **rum**

Mix well and let soak while you prepare the topping.

For the TOPPING

Put in food processor

¾ c.	**brown sugar**, lightly packed before measuring
½ c.	**flour**
½ tsp.	**cinnamon**
pinch	**salt**

Pulse briefly until mixed. Add

6 Tbs.	**butter**, very cold, cut in chunks

Pulse about **15 seconds** until ingredients begin to make small clumps.

Add	½ c.	**oats**
(Optional)	½ c.	**pecans** or **walnuts**, broken into pieces

Pulse briefly, just enough to mix.

Spread cherry mix on bottom of dish. Sprinkle topping over it. Bake about **50 minutes**. When cool, cut into squares and serve with heavy cream or vanilla ice cream.

MICROWAVED APPLE CRISP
(Serves 2)

From your arsenal   **2 individual microwave-safe bowls**

Peel, slice thickly and put in bowls

1 large or 2 small **apples**

Combine and sprinkle on apples

2 Tbs.	**oats**, quick-cooking if possible
2 Tbs.	**walnuts**, chopped
1 Tbs.	**brown sugar**
⅛ tsp.	**cinnamon**
2 tsp.	**butter** or **margarine**, cut into small pieces

Microwave on High for **4 to 5 minutes**. Let stand a few minutes. Serve lukewarm with **cream** or **vanilla ice cream**.

CLAFOUTIS

A *clafoutis* is like a baked upside-down crêpe with fruit. It is a lovely dessert and an excellent way to use up bits and pieces of fruit. The classic *clafoutis* is made with cherries, but other firm fruit or berries work well, too. You just spread the fruit pieces on the bottom of a buttered baking dish, pour a light crêpe batter over it, and bake it in a medium oven. Best served warm.

BASIC *CLAFOUTIS* RECIPE
(For 3 cups of fruit)

Preheat oven to **350°** F.

Put in blender in this order and blend at top speed for 1 minute

1½ c.	**milk***
⅓ c.	**sugar**
3	**eggs**
1 Tbs.	**vanilla**
pinch	**salt**
⅓ c.	**flour**

Butter a pie plate and spread with

3 c.	**fruit**, cut up

Pour on the above mixture. Bake for about **45 minutes**. The top should be browned and the *clafoutis* slightly puffed. Serve warm.

* Depending on what fruit you are using, you can mix the milk with **juices** from the fruit. For pears, apples, or plums you can marinate them in liqueur for an hour and combine the liquid with the milk.

NOTE: This recipe lends itself to smaller proportions. Use ½ c. milk, 1 egg, 1 tsp. vanilla, and 2 Tbs. each of flour and sugar for every cup of fruit.

PIES

A good way to use up over-the-hill fruit is to make a pie. Apples, peaches, and pears are the most likely candidates.

THIS MOM'S APPLE PIE

A bag of apples can last a long time, but sometimes a few start spoiling, and so emergency plans are called for. What could be more logical than good old apple pie? I have been using this method for so long that I never measure, so the measurements are approximate. It's best to leave yourself plenty of time so that the apples have time to steep. Also, if you are making your own pastry dough, it will need time to chill.

For the PASTRY

Prepare pastry dough for two crusts according to the procedure on page 51. Add 2 Tbs. **sugar** to the dry ingredients. Put in fridge to keep cold. If you have some in the freezer, remove and thaw while you prepare the filling.

For the FILLING

Peel, core, cut into fairly thin slices, and place in large bowl

| 6 large | **apples** |

If some are bruised, you will need to adjust the number. You should have about 4 cups of slices.

Stir in	⅓ c.	**brown sugar**, packed
	½ tsp.	**cinnamon**
	¼ tsp.	**powdered ginger**
		zest of 1 lemon
	1 Tbs.	**flour**
	¼ tsp.	**salt**
	1 Tbs.	**lemon juice** or **white wine**
(Optional)	¼ c.	**walnuts**, chopped

Stir these ingredients gently until well mixed and allow them to rest for ½ hour or more.

To ASSEMBLE

For homemade dough, cut dough ball in half and place one of the halves on a floured surface. Roll to desired shape and line the bottom of a standard pie dish with it. For the top crust, roll out the other half and cut strips about ¾ inch wide to make a lattice top. I prefer this method because, besides being pretty, it allows more moisture to escape during the baking process.

Preheat oven to **400°** F.

Pour the apple mixture into the pastry-lined pie dish and top with
2 oz. (½ stick) **butter**, cut into pieces

Cover with pastry strips in a woven pattern. Squeeze the ends into the lower crust and press with a fork all around the pie. Brush strips with **milk** or a spare **egg white** and sprinkle with a little **sugar**. If you prefer to leave the top crust whole, cut slits into it to allow steam to escape.

Put on lower shelf in oven and bake **40 to 50 minutes**. Poke a knife into the apples to make sure they are soft.

It's a good idea to put some aluminum foil under the pie dish or to place the pie dish on a baking sheet in case it bubbles over. Also, if the crust starts to burn before the apples are cooked, cover lightly with aluminum foil.

NOTE: This recipe can be adapted to **peaches**, using **granulated sugar** instead of brown and chopped or slivered **almonds** instead of walnuts.

PEAR TART

This is a one-crust pie with the slices of fruit arranged in an overlapping concentric pattern. The crust is partially baked before filling and then baked plain or with a custard topping.

Preheat oven to **400°** F.

For a PARTIALLY-BAKED CRUST

Line a 9-inch pie plate with a pie crust (see page 51 for homemade) and prick it in several places with a fork.

Grease the bottom of another same-sized pie plate and place on top. If it is heavy, like a Pyrex dish, continue to the next step. Otherwise, fill with a one-inch layer of dried beans or pie crust weights. If you don't have another same-sized pie plate, grease a sheet of aluminum foil and press it against the crust before adding the beans or weights.

Bake for **15 minutes** on the middle oven shelf. Allow to cool before filling.

For the FILLING

Peel, core, and cut into medium-thick slices

	6	**pears**

Arrange them on the pie crust in concentric circles.

Sprinkle with	⅓ c.	**sugar**
		zest of 1 lemon
	2 tsp.	**lemon juice**
	¼ tsp.	**cinnamon**
(Optional)	1 Tbs.	**white wine** (in this case, omit lemon juice)
Dot with	1 Tbs.	**butter**

Put on upper oven shelf and bake for about **40 minutes**, until fruit is soft and light brown.

PEAR TART VARIATION, with CUSTARD TOPPING

This tart is especially good. After baking for about 20 minutes, remove from oven and cover with the following custard mix.

In a bowl, beat together

	1	**egg**
	¼ c.	**sugar**
	2 Tbs.	**flour**
	½ c.	**half & half**
(Optional)	1 Tbs.	**pear brandy**

Pour this mixture over the partially-baked pie and bake for about **20 more minutes**, until the custard is puffy and lightly browned.

NOTE: This custard version of a fruit tart is equally good made with **apples**. You can substitute brown sugar if you like and Calvados for the pear brandy.

SWEET CRÊPES

Use the **fruit filling** on page 162 to make sweet stuffed crêpes. Instead of baking the fruit with a crumble topping, stew it gently for about **30 minutes** until it reaches a consistency to spread.

Meanwhile make sweet crêpes according to the recipe on page 61.

Spread the crêpes with the filling to within about an inch from the edges. Roll up the crêpe and place seam side down on a platter. Dust with sifted confectioners' sugar. Serve lukewarm or cold.

———————

COULIS

Coulis is another word for fruit syrup. Use it on pancakes, waffles, or to enhance puddings and cakes. Although it is not made from leftovers, it is pleasant to use with dishes that you *have* made with leftovers. Use berries, as suggested. Most other fruit is too bland.

RASPBERRY COULIS
(Makes about 1½ cups)
Put in small, heavy pan
             12 oz. thawed **frozen raspberries**
             ½ c.   **sugar**

Boil mixture uncovered over medium heat until it is reduced to a syrup consistency, about **20 minutes**. Strain to remove seeds. Cool to room temperature before serving.

Pour over pudding or cake slices.

NOTE: Frozen **blueberries** or **blackberries** also make a nice *coulis*. Mash them as they simmer. If you like, add ¼ tsp. **cinnamon** to the blueberries.

NOTE: Instead of frozen fruit, of course you can use fresh berries. This is a good solution if you need to rescue them before they spoil.

———————

COOKED FRUIT

STEWED FRUIT

You may have some fruit that needs to be dealt with before it spoils, such as apples, pears, peaches. Peel it and cut into halves, quarters, or slices. Make a syrup from a 2:1 ratio of water to sugar and poach the fruit in it.

(Serves about 4)

In a saucepan, stir, bring to boil, and simmer for 5 minutes

	2 c.	**water**
	1 c.	**sugar**
	pinch	**salt**
Add	3 to 4 c.	**fruit**, peeled and cut into pieces

Simmer for a few minutes till the fruit is soft. Remove with a slotted spoon to a bowl or dessert cups.

Continue simmering the syrup until it reduces to a fairly thick consistency. Pour onto fruit. Let cool, cover, and put in fridge till serving time.

Serve it chilled, garnished with a few blueberries or strawberries, or a spoonful of jam.

NOTE: Here are some optional additions to the water and sugar solution: **honey**, **wine**, **cinnamon**, **cloves**, **lemon juice**, **lemon zest**.

APPLE OR PEAR SAUCE

Another way to deal with over-the-hill apples or pears is to cook them, mash them, add some spices and serve cold over ice cream or plain cake, or spice cake (page 154).

Wash, quarter, and remove seeds, but leave skin on

apples and/or **pears**

Put in a large saucepan and add

half as much	**water**
1 to 2 Tbs.	**lemon juice**

Cook over low to medium heat until soft, adding water if necessary to prevent sticking.

Strain through a food mill (a.k.a. a ricer) or a coarse sieve.

Return the purée to the saucepan and bring slowly to a simmer.

Add	**sugar** to taste
¼ tsp.	**cinnamon**

Simmer for about **5 minutes**. Cool and store in refrigerator.

BAKED BANANAS

Mushy bananas are no fun to eat fresh, but they are divine baked and served as a warm dessert. This method is *so* easy and fast!

Preheat oven to **350° F.**

Butter	**an ovenproof dish**

Slice lengthwise and lay in dish round side up

	overripe bananas
Pour on some	**orange juice**
Sprinkle with	**sugar**
Dot with	**butter**

Put in oven till browned, **20 to 25 minutes**. Or you can broil them about **10 minutes** till browned. Serve lukewarm.

FRUIT TIMBALES

(Serves 4)

Set oven to **325° F** and place a pan with a rack and about one inch of water in it. If you don't have a rack that will fit into your pan, fold a towel into several layers and place on bottom of pan before filling with water.

Grease **4 ramekins or a medium-sized mold**
Put 1½ inches of water in a large **oven-proof pan**, put a **rack or a folded towel** in it and place in oven to heat.

Simmer until cooked through and put aside

1 c.	**fruit**, peeled and cut up
1 Tbs.	**butter**

Warm in microwave oven and put aside

1 c.	**half & half** (or a cream and syrup mix)

Beat together in a bowl

	3	**eggs**
	½ tsp.	**salt**
	1 Tbs.	**sugar**
Add	half	**the warmed half & half**

Add the cooked fruit.
Add other half of the warm cream. Mix well.

Pour mixture into buttered mold or ramekins. Remove the pan from the oven and place the ramekins or mold on the rack in the simmering water. Bake till custard is set, about **30 to 50 minutes**, depending on the size of the mold(s).

To unmold, run a knife around the edge and invert on serving plate.

FRUIT BREADS

BANANA BREAD

You probably have your own good recipe for banana bread, since it's an all-time favorite. The nice thing about it is that your mushy, overripe bananas can have such an elegant funeral. Here's a simple and very good recipe. And remember, if the bread gets stale, use it to make a cream dessert (Chapter 28, page 149).

Preheat oven to **350°** F.
Grease heavily **a 4- x 8-inch loaf pan**

Sift together and put aside
	1½ c.	**flour**
	2 tsp.	**baking powder**

In a large bowl, beat
	3 oz (¾ stick)	**butter** or **margarine**, softened
	½ c.	**sugar**
Beat in	1	**egg**
Mix in		**zest of 1 orange**
		zest of 1 lemon

Sprinkle in the flour mix and beat well.

Mash and add	2 to 3	**bananas** (about 1 cup)
Add	¼ c.	**walnuts**, chopped

Mix gently but thoroughly. Pour into prepared loaf pan. Bake for **1¼ hours**, but check after an hour. An inserted wooden toothpick should come out clean.

Let cool a little before turning out onto a rack.

NOTE: You can add some chopped dates, raisins, or dried apricots for variety.

BANANA and PECAN MUFFINS (From *Bread,* by Beth Hensberger)

These are sweet and very good and another great way to finish those mushy
bananas.

(Makes 12 muffins)

Preheat oven to **375°** F.
Grease or line with baking cups   **a 12-cup muffin pan**

In a large bowl, beat

	2	**eggs**
Slowly beat in	1 c.	**sugar**
Add and beat	½ c.	**vegetable oil**
Mash and beat in	1⅓ c.	**overripe bananas** (about 3 medium)
Chop fine and stir in ½ c.		**pecans**

In another bowl, sift together

2 c.	**flour**
1 tsp.	**baking powder**
1 tsp.	**baking soda**
½ tsp.	**cinnamon**
¼ tsp.	**salt**

Fold the flour mixture into the egg/banana mixture with as few strokes as
possible.

Pour into muffin cups and bake for about **25 minutes.**

Let cool a few minutes to set before removing to rack.

—————————————

AFTERWORD

Now that you have tried a few of these recipes, I hope that you have been inspired to look at those pesky containers of leftovers as treasures to be mined. Perhaps you have been able to make a delicious curry from that bit of leftover roast pork, augmenting it with lots of steamed rice, enough to feed your family one more memorable meal. Or, hopefully, you have resisted the temptation to chuck that bowl of cold mashed potatoes and have converted them into a covering for a succulent shepherd's pie. Or were you able to salvage some leftover spinach or peas or carrots or green beans, combine them with a few scraps of ham, and create attractive timbales as a first course for your dinner guests? If so, you, too, have become a queen (or king) of leftovers!

When you have learned the true value of the cooked food filed away in your refrigerator, you will look at your leftovers in a brand new way. You might even plan your food shopping accordingly, cooking, say, a roast one evening with the idea of a streamlined creamed dish the next night. A béchamel sauce is *so* easy and quick to make and will rescue an infinite number of leftovers. All you have to worry about is the accompanying starch (pasta, couscous, potatoes, rice, etc.) and a salad.

Dessert, of course, is another matter, and requires a separate block of time to prepare. However, you have seen how you can stretch your budget by salvaging sour milk, stale bread and cake, and over-the-hill fruit. Preparing pie crusts ahead of time and freezing them in aluminum pans all ready to go will save you time when quiches, pot pies, or fruit pies are on the menu. Cream desserts made with stale sweet breads are also better when made ahead of time.

THE REFRIGERATOR FILES

So the next time you open that refrigerator door and see all those containers of leftovers beckoning to you, I hope you will respond with a smile in anticipation of saving money and having fun being creative!

ANNEX 1

Suggestions for a holiday dinner's leftovers

THE TURKEY

Almost all the recommendations for Chicken listed in the Foretaste Interactive Guide apply. However, the old favorites are **Turkey Soup** (see the Soup chapter, page 28), followed closely by **Turkey Pot Pie** (see page 87). Equally good are the Mexican dishes recommended in Chapter 13, page 69. Also, turkey lends itself to a good **curry**, page 96. Turkey and mushroom **crêpes** are delicious (page 61).

THE GIBLETS

Use the heart and liver; save the gizzard and neck for the soup pot. Chop and sauté them in butter or olive oil along with some minced onions or *mirepoix* (see page 12). Add them to white sauces, gravies, or make a dip (see page 18), or you can use the liver to make Liver Pâté or the heavenly Mock Pâté de Foie Gras (see page 21).

THE MASHED POTATOES and SWEET POTATOES

See the recommendations in Chapters 22 (Potatoes) and 14 (Fritters and Croquettes). My favorite is **Shepherd's Pie** (Chapter 18, page 90).

THE VEGETABLES

See "Vegetables" in the Foretaste Interactive Guide on page xxi. I personally prefer leftover cold, cooked vegetables in **salads** made with homemade mayonnaise, with or without hard-boiled eggs, and accompanied by tomato slices and/or cucumber spears.

THE GRAVY

Add the gravy to your white sauces when you are making a creamed chicken or turkey dish. Put it in the soup you are making with the carcass.

BREAD or ROLLS

Please refer to Chapter 26 (Bread, page 137), Chapter 27 (Sweet Puddings, page 146), and Chapter 28 (Cream Desserts, page 149).

CAKE

Besides making crumbs, you can use slices of stale cake to make Cream Desserts (Chapter 28, page 149) or a Baked Alaska (Chapter 29, page 155).

ANNEX 2

What to buy on the weekend so you'll have plenty left over for the week

Since we're way too busy to go to the store more than once or twice a week, and since the wholesalers and big boxes offer such great bargains when buying in bulk, here are a few suggestions about what to load up on. You are probably doing this already anyway, but here goes. Please refer to the Foretaste Interactive Guide, page xxi, for more suggestions. Also, check the "Stand-bys" list on page 2.

MEAT and SEAFOOD

This is the single biggest money-saver. Watch for savings on **ham**. A large one will go on and on, providing you with endless dishes and sandwiches for your bagged lunch.

Pot roast will give back in multiple forms: Mexican dishes, pastas, turnovers, croquettes, etc. See in the Foretaste Interactive Guide under Meat, page xxiv.

A very large **chicken** has endless possibilities for adaptation. Again, see the Foretaste index, page xxii.

If you like lamb, plan a big meal around a **leg of lamb** and use up the leftovers as suggested in the Foretaste index under Meat, page xxiv. Stock made from the bones can be used to moisten the meat mixture in Shepherd's Pie or to cook barley. Cold slices with homemade mayonnaise make wonderful sandwiches. You can combine pieces with eggplant slices for a delicious baked dish. Then there's the sublime Moussaka (see page 91). Lamb is particularly good in curry.

A large **pork roast** will feed a crowd many times over. When you first roast it, you can put quarters of apples that need using up around it. See in the Foretaste Interactive Guide under Meat, page xxiv.

Large bags of **frozen shrimp, scallops, fish filets** often go on sale. Load up on them for quick defrosting to round out a leftover recipe. For example, make a large batch of seafood pasta sauce one evening and use the rest in a scalloped dish, a quiche, or for stuffed crêpes a day or two later.

VEGETABLES

Cooked vegetables are so handy to have around. Therefore buy large bags of frozen, so you have enough left over to work with. Some are cheaper and just as easy to buy fresh, such as carrots, broccoli, beets, turnips, and anything in the cabbage family. A large bag of fresh carrots is relatively cheap and will serve in many dishes. The same goes for a big bunch of celery. However, try to keep the celery as dry as possible by wrapping paper towel around it. A big bag of yellow onions is also a must in your arsenal.

FRUIT

Fruit is a chancy game, as its window of edibility is sometimes rather narrow. Buy bags of reliable fruit, like **grapefruit**, **oranges**, or **apples** that you can use as a base for a fruit salad into which you can sneak some pieces of over-the-hill fruit. **Bananas** are the great catalyst for a successful fruit salad and can be used in cake, dessert, or even soup (see page 32) recipes when they get mushy. And don't forget **kiwis**, which keep a long time and add nice color to your fruit salad. Mix in a little **honey, maple syrup**, or **agave syrup** to enhance the flavor.

BIBLIOGRAPHY

Here is a short list of the books that have been the most useful in assembling this collection of recipes for *The Refrigerator Files*. A few are recent discoveries, but many are old friends whose treasures I have shamelessly mined over the years.

Betty Crocker's Cookbook (Golden Press, 1972)

Child, Julia; Bertholle, Louisette; Beck, Simone, ***Mastering the Art of French Cooking*** (Alfred A. Knopf, Inc., 1961)

Child, Julia, ***Julia's Kitchen Wisdom*** (Alfred A. Knopf, 2009)

Rombauer, Irma S.; Becker, Marion Rombauer, ***Joy of Cooking*** (The Bobbs-Merrill Co., Inc., 1952 & 1973)

Goldstein, Darra, ***A Taste of Russia***, (Russian Life Books, 1999, second edition)

Hensperger, Beth, ***Bread*** (Chronicle Books, 1988)

Herbst, Sharon Tyler, ***The New Food Lover's Companion*** (Barron's, 2007, fourth edition)

Montagné, Prosper, ***The New Larousse Gastronomique*** (Crown Publishers, Inc., 1977, American edition)

Smith, Delia, ***Delia Smith's Complete Cookery Course*** (BBC Books, 1993)

INDEX

HOW TO ORDER THIS BOOK

If you would like more copies of this book, *THE REFRIGERATOR FILES, Creative Makeovers for your Leftovers* by Jocelyn Deprez, you may Google the iUniverse Publishing Company's Web site:

iUniverse.com

From Google's official iUniverse.com site
Click on   **Bookstore**
Click on   **Advanced Search**
Fill in box for   **Title**
Click on   **Search**
Scroll down to see result.
Click on title for more details.
Proceed to Check-out by clicking on
                                                 Add to Cart.

You can also visit your local **Barnes and Noble** store or go to their Web site at **barnesandnoble.com**.

You can also find us on **Amazon.com**.

ABOUT THE AUTHOR

Jocelyn Deprez has walked the walk from total novice to chief family chef. Barely able to boil an egg when she married, she has survived a fifty-year apprenticeship in putting a decent meal on the table for her husband and four children. Early years of living on a shoestring taught her thrift. There seemed to be a never-ending supply of cooked food to be used up, presenting a daily challenge to the imagination.

Born in Canada of American and English parents, a childhood spent moving about Europe and the United States, evacuation from England to Cleveland, Ohio, during World War II, two college years spent in Switzerland, all have given Jocelyn an international outlook and an appreciation for diversity. Majoring in German at Smith College, raising a family in Connecticut, Paris, and Switzerland, she has picked up cooking techniques from diverse sources. Subsequently teaching French and English for twenty-two years, time in the kitchen had to be adjusted to her busy schedule. This situation is not unlike most of the women out there in the working world who need to feed a family on a short budget and even shorter schedule.

Now that she has retired with her husband to Orlando, Florida, her kitchen duties fluctuate from cooking for large family gatherings to experimenting with tasty tidbits for two. To get out of the kitchen, Jocelyn likes to read history and foreign affairs, dig in the garden, and attend the ballet.

Ever more conscious of the financial challenges of today's families, Jocelyn has decided to write down some of her ideas about making food stretch and, most of all, enhancing it in the process. This book is not about yet another collection of exotic recipes. It's about common sense and using what you have on hand to create basic and tasty meals for the whole family.